ROMANTIC ITALIAN COOKERY

ROMANTIC
ITALIAN COOKERY

Mary Cadogan

CONTENTS

First published in 1985 by Octopus Books Limited
59 Grosvenor Street, London W1

© 1984 Hennerwood Publications Limited

ISBN 0 86273 117 8

Produced by Mandarin Publishers Limited
22a Westlands Road
Quarry Bay
Hong Kong
Printed in Hong Kong

INTRODUCTION

As restaurant eating becomes increasingly expensive, so entertaining at home grows in popularity. There are many advantages besides economy: it is easier to relax and talk freely without any neighbour to eavesdrop or waiter to interrupt you; and there's no rush to vacate your table at the end of the meal.

Choosing the menu
The first step in planning an enjoyable dinner for two is to decide on a menu that will suit your taste and that of your guest, and reflect the mood you wish to create. The amount of preparation involved is another consideration, as is the budget, too.

The menu itself can be as simple or elaborate as you wish, but avoid too many recipes where last minute cooking is required. The more you can prepare in advance, the more relaxed and confident you will feel. Check also that your menu will not over-use equipment or oven space.

You could serve just one beautifully prepared and presented main course followed by a delicious array of fruit and cheeses, or several smaller courses providing flavour and colour contrasts. You will find that many of the pasta, rice and pizza recipes, and some of the vegetables and salads, serve equally well as starters or as part of a main course, although quantities may be reduced if you choose one of these dishes for a starter. Most of the vegetable recipes are fairly generous, to allow for second servings. Whatever you decide on, try to balance the courses so that they are not too filling. For example if you opt for a pasta dish starter, offer a light main course. A vegetable or salad starter can be followed by a rather more substantial dish.

Here is a menu suggestion with taste, colour and texture balanced to give an enjoyable dinner.

Parma Ham with Avocado
Stuffed Chicken Breasts
Pilaf Rice with Cèpe Mushrooms
Green Salad
Strawberry Water Ice
Selection of Cheeses
Coffee

In this menu the starter, main dish, salad and dessert can be prepared several hours ahead, and the rice is quick to cook and needs little attention. The pink and green starter contrasts with the lighter coloured main course, while the dessert provides a fresh taste to round off the meal. Cheese could be optional.

Planning the preparation
A good suggestion when organizing your preparation is to work out a time plan. Make a note of when each dish should start being prepared and cooked, and when to remove it from the oven or freezer. Also allow a little time between each course. Write the times as a countdown and display it in the kitchen, remembering to give yourself plenty of time to set the table and to get changed.

If you can, try to clear up as you go along, otherwise you may find that you run out of saucepans and implements if they are all stacked in the sink, let alone space for working. Leave plenty of time to clear the decks before your guest arrives.

Keeping food warm
You may like to invite your guest into the kitchen, whilst you put the finishing touches to the main course. Even so it is helpful to have completed most of the preparation before your guest arrives. Most of the food in this book will keep warm for the time taken to welcome your guest and to enjoy the first course.

Many of the main dishes can be covered tightly with a lid or foil and kept warm in a cool to moderate oven. Fish tends to dry out slightly without special care and to prevent this wrap the fish in foil, then place it on a rack above a shallow covering of hot water in a roasting pan. (Fish which is breaded will not suit this technique.)

Most sauces can be partly or completely prepared before the first course, and reheated gently before serving. Although an undressed salad can be covered with cling film and stored in the refrigerator for a few hours, dress salads only at the last minute.

If you wish to cook pasta ahead of time, drain it and leave it to cool. When ready to serve, plunge it back into boiling salted water, stirring it for 1-2 minutes, then drain it again thoroughly. Cooked rice can be kept warm in the oven, covered with damp greaseproof paper.

The drinks
It helps to have aperitifs on hand ready to serve with plenty of ice and slices of orange or lemon. Chill the wine if it is white, and pull the cork on red wine 1-2 hours before serving it, or pour red wine into an attractive decanter. See page 9 for advice on Italian wines. If you serve a sparkling wine which is not a Champagne try frosting the glasses with sugar (page 70).

The cheeseboard

A good-looking cheeseboard need consist of only two or three delicious Italian cheeses. Take them out of the refrigerator and unwrap them an hour or so before serving. The cheese can be arranged on a plate or board garnished with a small bunch of grapes, a few sprigs of watercress, orange wedges or fresh herbs. Serve biscuits in a basket lined with a napkin and curls or small squares of butter in a chilled dish.

Serving coffee

Well-made coffee provides a perfect end to a meal. The Italians drink small cups of strong black caffè espresso, or frothy, milky caffè cappuccino using a dark roasted coffee. If you don't own a caffettiera, a napoletana or a moka, which are all Italian-style coffee pots, filter coffee is the nearest equivalent. Choose a blend of coffee to suit your taste, avoiding the lighter roasted thin coffees. Vienna coffee and Mocha blends are two worth trying. To make frothy caffè cappuccino heat the milk and whizz it in the liquidizer or with an electric whisk for a few seconds. Pour the milk over the black coffee and sprinkle with drinking chocolate. Caffè corretto, coffee laced with a liqueur or brandy, could also be served with a few Amaretto di Saronno macaroons, or thin wedges of Panforte, an Italian sweetmeat.

The cook's tools

No special equipment is needed to prepare these recipes, but you might find the following useful:

Food processor/Liquidizer: for puréeing soups and sauces, making breadcrumbs, grating cheese, chopping herbs, and a thousand other little jobs.
Electric whisk: for whipping cream and egg whites, making sorbet, whisking egg yolks and sugar together.
Nutmeg grater: useful for obtaining the best flavour from this spice.
Draining spoon: for removing fried food from fat. Do not use a wire basket for food in batter, such as Fritto misto (page 50), for it tends to stick to the wire mesh.
Pestle and mortar: for crushing garlic, making green sauce and dressings, bruising spices such as juniper berries and mixing small quantities.

The cook's special ingredients

Italian ingredients are becoming increasingly available in high street supermarkets and delicatessens. Here are the ones you are likely to need or may like to try, with substitutes where appropriate.

Cheeses

Bel Paese: a soft, creamy, melting cheese. Used as a table cheese and for cooking. It can be used instead of Mozzarella for pizza toppings, salads, etc.
Fontina: a semi-hard cheese with a sweet, nutty flavour and creamy texture. Eaten as a table cheese and as a good melting cheese in cooked dishes, such as the Fonduta piemontese (page 12).
Gorgonzola: a mild, blue-veined cheese from Lombardy. Dolcelatte is a creamy type of Gorgonzola.

THE CHEESEBOARD: CLOCKWISE FROM TOP: Bel Paese; Gorgonzola; Fontina; Pecorino

ON CIRCULAR MARBLE: CLOCKWISE FROM RIGHT: Cotechino sausage; Mozzarella; Basil; Brassaola; Salame napoletana; Salame milanese; Mortadella; Prosciutto di Parma. IN FRONT: Salsicce linked together; plain (left) and with peppers (right)

Mozzarella: this moist, waxy cheese is commonly used as a pizza topping although it has many other uses. It can be fried, baked, and used in salads.

Parmesan (Parmigiano): the most famous of all Italian cheeses, Parmesan is a matured hard cheese. It is finely grated and used in countless Italian dishes. Try to buy Parmesan cheese in a piece from large supermarkets and delicatessens and grate it yourself; the flavour is far superior to the ready-grated variety in packets.

Pecorino: this hard, mature sheep's milk cheese makes a good, but sharper, alternative to Parmesan, and is excellent for grating and cooking with pasta. Fresh pecorino is light in colour and soft textured. It is delicious added to the cheeseboard.

Ricotta: a soft, white, crumbly cheese which is used for both sweet and savoury dishes. It has a bland, slightly salty flavour. If you are unable to buy ricotta, use drained and sieved curd or cottage cheese.

Cured meats and sausages

Bresaola: dry cured, beef fillet cut into wafer-thin slices. Served as an antipasto sprinkled with olive oil, pepper and lemon wedges to squeeze.

Cotechin: a spicy pork sausage which can be boiled and served with hot vegetables, or sliced and served cold.

Mortadella: the largest Italian cured sausage. Made with pork and spices and studded with pork fat. Served cold thinly sliced, or diced for cooking.

Prosciutto di Parma (Parma ham): delicately cured ham eaten in wafer-thin slices. Good with figs or melon. No substitute.

Salame: there are numerous types of Italian salame, the most commonly available being Salame milanese, Salame napoletana and Salame genovese. These all tend to be coarse-textured and lightly seasoned. Serve a small quantity with olives as a simple antipasto.

Salsicce: fresh meaty sausages for grilling or frying. Usually made of pork, some are peppery hot while others are only mildly flavoured. There are countless names given to various types but in Italy Salsiccia al metro is sold by the metre, hence its name. Salamelle is often the same mixture tied into links with string. Another type is Luganeghe.

Herbs

These play an important part in many Italian dishes. Fresh herbs have the best flavour and are becoming easier to buy if you do not grow your own. Those most commonly used are basil, bay leaves, oregano or marjoram, parsley (try English for cooking and prettier Continental parsley for garnishing), rosemary and sage.

Garlic is used throughout Italy. The flavour can be modified to suit your taste, except in dishes such as Pesto (page 13), and Bagna cauda (page 16), which rely heavily on garlic flavour. Pink-skinned garlic tends to have a sweeter flavour than the white.

Cèpe mushrooms

Wild mushrooms such as cèpes can be bought in the autumn. They are used in sauces, rice dishes, soups, omelettes and many other dishes. When not available use dried mushrooms which have a rich, concentrated flavour. Soak them for 30 minutes in warm water, then drain them and slice thinly, ready for use.

Olive oil

In southern Italy olive oil is used extensively for cooking. Northern Italians favour butter for cooking and in Central Italy they use a mixture of both! Buy the best olive oil you can afford as cheap oil is a false economy when it is overpowering in flavour.

Pine nuts

These distinctive nuts are the seeds of the pine cone. They are used in meat and game dishes, particularly in stuffings, and sweet and sour sauces (page 55). Buy them from larger supermarkets and health food shops.

Rice

Italian rice is thicker and shorter grained than American or long grain rice. The texture of the cooked rice is creamy, in contrast to long grain rice which is dry and fluffy. Arborio rice and 'Easy cook' Italian rice are available in most supermarkets.

Pasta

There are as many varieties of pasta as there are ways of serving it. There's green pasta and wholemeal pasta; you can buy it dried, stuffed, fresh and frozen, in countless shapes and sizes. There is, however, only one proper way of cooking it and it is very simple. Dried pasta will take longer to cook than fresh or frozen and different shapes of pasta will vary in their cooking time, too. 'Al dente' means firm to the bite and this is how Italians eat their pasta. Check the pasta by trying a small piece after the minimum cooking time, to avoid overcooking it.

To cook pasta, bring a large saucepan of water to the boil. Use about 4 litres (7 pints) for every 450 g (1 lb) of pasta. Add 1 tablespoon of salt. When the water is rapidly boiling add the pasta all at once. (Feed long pasta into the pan as it softens.) Stir the pasta with a large wooden spoon to prevent it sticking together, then cook it, uncovered. Drain the pasta quickly once it is cooked, shaking the colander to remove excess water. Add a knob of butter or a little grated Parmesan cheese (or both) (see page 31).

Tomatoes

Juicy ripe tomatoes make the best sauces when they are in season. In winter use canned Italian tomatoes for a good flavour. Don't use fresh tomatoes in winter, for there is just not enough flavour in them. To thicken and enrich sauces, add the concentrated flavour of tomato purée. A pinch of sugar or honey added to tomato dishes helps to balance the flavour.

Marsala

This fortified wine is used extensively in Italian cooking, mainly for desserts but also for some savoury dishes. Choose dry or medium Marsala for cooking, but avoid Egg Marsala (Marsala all'uovo) which is a sticky dessert wine, unsuitable for cooking.

Your own wine guide

With each of the meat, poultry and fish recipes we have given a suggestion for wine. Here is a selection of Italian wines which fit into each of those categories. You will find that many of the wines are available from various food stores, as well as wine merchants.

Robust red wines
Barbera d'Asti
Barolo
Nebbiolo
Venegazzu
Brunello di Montalcino
Cabernet Grave del Fruili
Valpolicella Amarone

Light red wines
Raboso del Veneto
Bardolino
Lambrusco – slightly sparkling and ranging from sweet to dry. Best served chilled.

Dry red wines
Chianti Classico
Barbaresco

Fruity medium red wines
Sangiovese di Romagna
Dolcetto

Fruity medium dry white wine
Orvieto Abboccato

Fruity dry white wines
Pinot Grigio
Tocai
Verdicchio

Light dry white wines
Soave
Verduzzo del Piave

Dry white wines
Orvieto
Frascati
Vernaccia

To round off the meal there are several Italian liqueurs to choose from:
Grappa – a fiery liqueur made from grape skins and pips, and generally flavoured with a plant called rue.
Maraschino – a sweet liqueur made from cherries.
Strega – a herby liqueur.
Amaretto di Saronno – a strong almond-flavoured liqueur.
Sambuca – a taste of anise.

SOUPS & STARTERS

SARDE FRITTE
Deep-fried paprika sardines

225 g (8 oz) fresh or frozen sardines, thawed if frozen
½ teaspoon salt
2 teaspoons paprika
2 teaspoons plain flour
oil, for deep frying
To garnish:
lemon slices
sprigs of parsley

Preparation time: 10 minutes
Cooking time: 3-4 minutes

1. Clean the sardines if necessary, wash inside and out and pat dry with paper towels.
2. Sift the salt, paprika and flour on to a plate. Roll the sardines in this mixture until well coated.
3. Heat the oil to 180°C/350°F or until a cube of bread browns in 30 seconds.
4. Fry the sardines for 3-4 minutes until crispy and golden. Drain on paper towels and serve with the lemon slices, garnished with parsley.

MOUSSE DI SALMONE
Salmon and herb mousse

50 g (2 oz) curd cheese or Petit Suisse
1 tablespoon lemon juice
1 × 90 g (3½ oz) can salmon, drained and flaked
salt
freshly ground black pepper
2 lettuce leaves
2 tablespoons finely chopped fresh mixed herbs, i.e. chives, tarragon, parsley, marjoram, basil

Preparation time: 15 minutes

1. Blend the curd cheese or Petit Suisse with the lemon juice, and add the flaked salmon, salt and pepper. [A]
2. Place a lettuce leaf on each serving plate and place a mound of mousse on each leaf. Sprinkle fine lines of chopped herbs over the mousse.

[A] The mousse can be prepared up to a couple of hours in advance and chilled until ready to serve.

INSALATA DI FRUTTI DI MARE
Seafood salad

½ small red pepper, cored and seeded
1 carrot
1 stick celery
a few lettuce leaves
1 small onion, peeled and thinly sliced
100 g (4 oz) peeled prawns
1 × 90 g (3½ oz) can tuna, drained and flaked
4 stuffed olives, sliced
Dressing:
3 tablespoons olive oil
1 tablespoon lemon juice
1 clove garlic, peeled and crushed
1 teaspoon fresh marjoram, chopped or ½ teaspoon dried marjoram
salt
freshly ground black pepper

Preparation time: 20 minutes

1. Cut the pepper into thin strips. Peel the carrot and cut into thin sticks. Cut the celery into sticks. Mix the pepper, carrot, celery and onion together. Make a bed of lettuce leaves and place the salad on 2 small dishes or plates.
2. Mix together the prawns, tuna and olives and arrange on the salad.
3. Place all the dressing ingredients in a screw-topped jar and shake well to mix. [A]
4. Pour the dressing over the salad to serve.

[A] Cover the salad with cling film and seal the dressing jar. Keep in the refrigerator for up to 8 hours.

Sarde fritte; Insalata di frutti di mare

FONDUTA PIEMONTESE
Piedmontese cheese fondue

150 ml (¼ pint) milk
175 g (6 oz) Fontina cheese, cut into small cubes
2 egg yolks
25 g (1 oz) butter
25 g (1 oz) button mushrooms, finely sliced
To serve:
French bread

Preparation time: 5 minutes
Cooking time: 25 minutes

Delicious as a fondue with French bread to dip into it, Fonduta may also be served with a spoon and enjoyed as a soup.

1. Heat the milk, then place in a bowl over hot water with the cheese and egg yolks.
2. Keep the water under the bowl gently bubbling and stir the sauce occasionally until it is smooth and the cheese has melted.
3. Stir in the butter until melted.
4. Divide the sauce between individual dishes and sprinkle with slices of mushroom. Serve with rounds of French bread as it is, or toasted.

MINESTRONE FREDDO CON PESTO
Cold minestrone with basil sauce

1 tablespoon olive oil
1 garlic clove, peeled and crushed
1 small aubergine, cubed
225 g (8 oz) tomatoes, skinned and chopped
1 courgette, sliced
1 tablespoon tomato purée
150 ml (¼ pint) water
salt
freshly ground black pepper
Pesto:
1 bunch fresh basil, finely chopped
2 garlic cloves, peeled
1 tablespoon finely chopped pine nuts
25 g (1 oz) Parmesan cheese, grated
4 tablespoons olive oil
To serve:
grated Parmesan cheese

Preparation time: 10 minutes, plus cooling
Cooking time: 15 minutes

Served cold, this starter has a similar texture and flavour to the French ratatouille. For a hearty winter soup it can also be served hot. Instead of making your own pesto, you can buy it in jars in many large supermarkets or delicatessens.

1. Heat the oil in a saucepan, add the garlic and fry gently for 1 minute.
2. Add the aubergine, tomatoes and courgette. Stir well, reduce the heat and cook, covered, for 5 minutes.
3. Add the tomato purée, water, salt and pepper. Bring to the boil, then simmer gently for about 5 minutes, until the vegetables are tender. [A]
4. Meanwhile make the pesto. Place the basil, garlic, nuts and cheese in a mortar or small liquidizer. Pound with a pestle or blend until the mixture is finely ground. Blend in the oil gradually. [A]
5. Pour the mixture into individual bowls and leave to cool. When cold, stir pesto into each bowl and sprinkle with Parmesan cheese.

[A] Make the minestrone up to 24 hours and the Pesto up to 1 week in advance and store in covered containers in the refrigerator.

Minestrone freddo con pesto; Fonduta piemontese; Minestra di pomodoro con odori

MINESTRA DI POMODORO CON ODORI
Tomato soup with herbs

1 tablespoon olive oil
1 small onion, peeled and finely chopped
1 small potato, peeled and finely chopped
1 garlic clove, peeled and crushed
450 g (1lb) tomatoes, skinned and chopped
½ teaspoon dried oregano
1 tablespoon chopped celery leaves
½ teaspoon dried basil
pinch of sugar
salt
freshly ground black pepper
Croûtons:
2 slices bread
4 tablespoons olive oil
To garnish:
Continental parsley

Preparation time: 20 minutes
Cooking time: 25-30 minutes

1. Heat the olive oil in a saucepan. Add the onion, potato and garlic and fry gently for 5 minutes, until the onion is softened.
2. Add the tomatoes to the pan with the oregano, celery leaves, basil, sugar, salt and pepper. Bring to the boil, then simmer, covered, for 15 minutes.
3. Liquidize or process the soup until smooth. [A] [F]
4. Return to the pan and reheat. Serve with croûtons.
5. To make croûtons, cut out four heart shapes from each slice of bread, using a small heart cutter or a very sharp knife.
6. Heat the oil in a frying pan, add the bread shapes and fry for a few minutes, turning once, until crisp and golden. Drain on paper towels.

[A] Make up to 24 hours in advance and store in a covered container in the refrigerator.
[F] Reheat the soup from frozen, stirring occasionally.

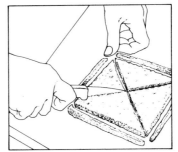
For heart-shaped croûtons, use a small, sharp knife and cut the crusts off a slice of bread. Cut the slice diagonally into 4.

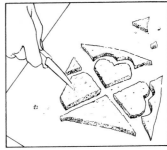
Make an indent along the outside edge and continue to cut round to make a heart shape.

MINESTRA ALL'ACETOSA
Sorrel soup

25 g (1 oz) butter
1 medium onion, peeled and chopped
225 g (8 oz) potatoes, peeled and chopped
salt
freshly ground black pepper
450 ml (¾ pint) chicken stock
100 g (4 oz) sorrel leaves, shredded
2 tablespoons single cream
2 teaspoons snipped chives

Preparation time: 10 minutes
Cooking time: 20 minutes

1. Melt the butter in a saucepan, add the onion and potatoes and cook gently, covered, for about 10 minutes, stirring occasionally.
2. Add salt, pepper and stock and bring to the boil. Simmer, uncovered, for about 5 minutes until the potatoes are tender.
3. Add the sorrel leaves and cook for 5 minutes more. Liquidize or process the soup until smooth. A F
4. Pour the soup into individual bowls and swirl a tablespoon of cream into each. Sprinkle with chives.

A Can be made the day before and stored in the refrigerator. Reheat gently before serving.
F Thaw overnight in the refrigerator, then reheat gently to avoid overcooking.

Variation
Zuppa di crescione (Watercress soup). Replace sorrel leaves with one bunch of watercress, trimmed and washed.

MINESTRA DI SPINACI E POLENTA
Spinach and polenta soup

50 g (2 oz) butter
1 garlic clove, peeled and crushed
450 g (1 lb) spinach, washed
3 pinches nutmeg
salt
freshly ground black pepper
1 tablespoon polenta
450 ml (¾ pint) chicken stock
4 tablespoons single cream

Preparation time: 10 minutes
Cooking time: 12-15 minutes

ZUPPA DI POLLO CON MARSALA
Chicken soup with Marsala

1 chicken portion
1 carrot, peeled and chopped
1 stick celery, chopped
2 cloves
1 cinnamon stick
1 medium onion, peeled
600 ml (1 pint) water
bouquet garni
2 egg yolks
4 tablespoons Marsala
25 g (1 oz) butter
grated nutmeg

Preparation time: 20 minutes
Cooking time: 1½ hours

1. Place the chicken in a saucepan with the carrot, celery, cloves, cinnamon, onion, water and bouquet garni. Bring to the boil, cover and simmer for 1 hour.
2. Strain the broth and cut a little of the chicken into thin strips. A F
3. Place the egg yolks in a bowl and beat in the Marsala and broth. Strain into a saucepan and cook gently, stirring, until just under boiling point. This will take about 15 minutes.
4. Stir in the butter, a piece at a time, cooking until the soup is thickened to a pouring consistency. Stir in the reserved strips of chicken and heat through.
5. Pour the soup into individual bowls and sprinkle with grated nutmeg.

A Store the stock and chicken separately in covered containers in the refrigerator for up to 24 hours.
F Reheat the broth gently from frozen and continue from step 3.

1. Melt the butter in a saucepan, add the garlic and fry for 1 minute.
2. Add the spinach, nutmeg, salt and pepper. Stir well, then cover and cook gently for 2 minutes. Stir in the polenta and stock and bring to the boil.
3. Simmer for 5 minutes, stirring occasionally, until the spinach is tender. Liquidize until smooth. A F
4. Reheat the soup gently and stir in the cream just before serving.

A Make up to 24 hours in advance and store in a covered container in the refrigerator.
F Thaw in the refrigerator, then reheat gently.

TOP TO BOTTOM: Minestra all'acetosa; Zuppa di pollo con Marsala

Frittata al dragoncello; Bagna cauda with selection of raw vegetables served separately; Crostate di spinaci e ricotta

FRITTATA AL DRAGONCELLO
Tarragon omelette

---

3 eggs
1 tablespoon single cream
1 tablespoon chopped fresh tarragon or 1 teaspoon dried
  tarragon
salt
freshly ground black pepper
25 g (1 oz) butter
To garnish:
tarragon sprigs

Preparation time: 5 minutes
Cooking time: 3-4 minutes

1. Beat together the eggs, cream, tarragon, salt and pepper.
2. Heat the butter in a frying pan until foaming. Pour in the egg mixture, tilting the pan to cover the base evenly.
3. Cook the omelette gently until almost set, then place under a preheated hot grill for 30 seconds to cook the top.
4. Garnish with tarragon and cut in half upon serving.

BAGNA CAUDA
Garlic and anchovy dip

---

1 × 50 g (2 oz) can anchovies
50 g (2 oz) butter
4 tablespoons olive oil
1 garlic clove, peeled and crushed
To serve:
Raw vegetables, e.g. courgette, celery or carrot sticks,
  radishes, slices of peppers, broccoli or cauliflower
  florets

Preparation time: 5 minutes
Cooking time: 10 minutes

This essentially peasant dish is best kept warm at the table in an earthenware pot over a nightlight.

1. Drain the anchovies and chop them finely.
2. Heat the butter and oil in a small saucepan, add the garlic and anchovies and simmer for 10 minutes.
3. Serve warm with chunks of bread or crisp vegetables to dip.

CROSTATE DI SPINACI E RICOTTA
Spinach and ricotta tartlets

50 g (2 oz) plain flour
pinch of salt
25 g (1 oz) butter
1 teaspoon water
Filling:
50 g (2 oz) frozen chopped spinach, thawed
100 g (4 oz) ricotta or curd cheese
2 teaspoons grated Parmesan cheese
2 pinches nutmeg
1 egg, beaten
2 tablespoons single cream
salt
freshly ground black pepper

Preparation time: 20 minutes
Cooking time: 30-35 minutes
Oven: 200°C, 400°F, Gas Mark 6

The quantity of pastry given is for two tartlets, but if you feel it is not worthwhile making such a small amount, you can double or quadruple the pastry ingredients and use the surplus to make a flan case which can then be frozen for a future occasion.

1. Place the flour and salt in a bowl. Add the butter, cut into small pieces, and rub in until the mixture resembles fine breadcrumbs.
2. Add the water and mix to a firm dough. Turn out on to a floured surface and knead lightly.
3. Divide the dough in half. Roll out each piece to line a 10 cm (4 inch) tartlet case. Place the cases on a baking sheet, prick the pastry with a fork and bake in a preheated oven for 10 minutes. A F
4. Place all the filling ingredients in a bowl and mix well. Pour into the pastry cases and return to the oven for a further 20-25 minutes until the filling has just set. Serve warm or cold.

A Store in a covered container for up to 24 hours.
F Fill frozen partly baked cases with spinach mixture and bake for an extra 5 minutes.

PEPERONI CON ALICI
Baked peppers with anchovies

1 green pepper
1 red pepper
2 garlic cloves, peeled and finely chopped
2 small tomatoes, sliced
4 anchovy fillets
2 tablespoons olive oil
To serve:
quartered lemon slices

Preparation time: 15 minutes
Cooking time: 40 minutes
Oven: 190°C, 375°F, Gas Mark 5

1. Place the whole peppers under the grill, turning occasionally until the skin is charred. Cool slightly, then remove the skin with a small sharp knife. Cut each pepper in quarters and remove the seeds.
2. Place the peppers on a greased baking sheet, skinned side down. Sprinkle with chopped garlic and arrange a slice of tomato over the top of each piece.
3. Halve each anchovy fillet crossways, then lengthways and arrange two pieces of anchovy over each tomato. Drizzle over the oil.
4. Bake in a preheated oven for 30 minutes until the peppers are just cooked. Serve hot or cold with lemon slices to garnish.

UOVA FARCITE DI PEPERONI
Eggs stuffed with peppers

2 eggs, hard-boiled
½ small red pepper
1 tablespoon olive oil
1 teaspoon capers, finely chopped
2 teaspoons finely chopped fresh parsley
1 anchovy fillet, finely chopped
½ teaspoon Dijon mustard
salt
freshly ground black pepper
To serve:
shredded lettuce

Preparation time: 15 minutes
Cooking time: 5 minutes

CLOCKWISE FROM TOP: Peperoni con alici; Uova farcite di peperoni; Prosciutto di Parma con avocado

PROSCIUTTO DI PARMA CON AVOCADO
Parma ham with avocado

1 ripe medium avocado
6 slices Parma ham, about 75 g (3 oz) together
Dressing:
1 tablespoon olive oil
1 teaspoon lemon juice
1 garlic clove, peeled and crushed
2 teaspoons chopped fresh parsley
salt
freshly ground black pepper

Preparation time: 10 minutes

1. Cut the avocado in half and remove the stone. Peel off the skin and cut each half into 3 thick slices.
2. Wrap each slice of ham around a slice of avocado. Arrange on a serving dish.
3. Place all the dressing ingredients in a screw-topped jar and shake well to mix.
4. Pour the dressing over the avocado to serve.

Variation
Prosciutto di Parma con fichi (Parma ham with figs). Serve 2 ripe figs per person, cutting each down through the centre in a cross. Open out the figs and arrange on the plates with the slices of Parma ham. Omit the dressing.

1. Cut the eggs in half and remove the yolks. Sieve the yolks into a bowl.
2. Plunge the pepper into a pan of boiling salted water and cook for 5 minutes. Drain and dry with a paper towel. Cut 8 strips from the pepper and finely chop the remainder.
3. Add the chopped pepper to the egg yolks with the olive oil, capers, parsley, anchovy, mustard, salt and pepper. Mix well.
4. Spoon the mixture into the egg white halves and top each with 2 strips of pepper in a cross.
5. Serve the eggs on a bed of shredded lettuce.

To check whether an avocado is ripe, cradle it in your hand and apply gentle pressure. If it gives very slightly the avocado is ripe. Avoid those that are very soft or have dark blemishes, as the flesh may have discoloured. To prevent an avocado becoming overripe, it can be kept in the refrigerator for a few days.

PASTA, PIZZA & RICE

RISOTTO DI GAMBERONI
Risotto with king prawns and brandy

450 ml (¾ pint) hot chicken stock
½ teaspoon saffron threads
75 g (3 oz) butter
1 small onion, peeled and chopped
100 g (4 oz) green beans, chopped into 2.5 cm (1 inch)
   lengths
175 g (6 oz) Italian rice
150 ml (¼ pint) white wine
50 g (2 oz) frozen peas
2 teaspoons snipped chives
1 teaspoon chopped fresh dill or ½ teaspoon dried dill
salt
freshly ground black pepper
2-3 teaspoons grated Parmesan cheese
small garlic clove, peeled and crushed
6 king prawns, shelled, with heads left on
2 tablespoons brandy
To garnish:
sprigs of dill

Preparation time: 20 minutes, plus soaking
Cooking time: 40 minutes

1. Pour the hot stock over the saffron threads and leave for about 30 minutes.
2. Melt 25 g (1 oz) butter in a saucepan, add the onion and fry gently for about 5 minutes, until softened. Add the beans and cook for 1 minute.
3. Add the rice and stir until all the grains are coated with butter. Add one third of the stock together with saffron threads and bring to the boil. Simmer, uncovered, until the stock is absorbed, then gradually add the remaining stock and white wine and continue cooking for about 20 minutes, until the rice is tender and the liquid absorbed. Add the peas 5 minutes before the end of this cooking time.
4. Stir in the chives, dill, salt, pepper, 25 g (1 oz) of the butter and the Parmesan cheese. Keep the rice warm while you prepare the prawns.
5. Heat the remaining butter in a frying pan and add the garlic. Cook for 1 minute, then add the prawns. Sprinkle with salt and pepper and cook for about 5 minutes, until heated through. Pour over the brandy and ignite.
6. Divide the rice between two serving dishes, or serve on a single dish, and place the prawns on top. Garnish with sprigs of dill.

ANELLO DI RISOTTO AI FEGATINI
Risotto ring with chicken liver sauce

25 g (1 oz) butter
1 small onion, peeled and finely chopped
175 g (6 oz) Italian rice
600 ml (1 pint) hot chicken stock
salt
freshly ground black pepper
Sauce:
3 tablespoons olive oil, for frying
1 garlic clove, peeled and crushed
1 small onion, peeled and chopped
1 small green pepper, cored, seeded and chopped
225 g (8 oz) chicken livers, roughly chopped
1 teaspoon tomato purée
4 tablespoons dry vermouth
2 tablespoons water
1 teaspoon chopped fresh sage or ½ teaspoon dried sage
To finish:
1 tablespoon grated Parmesan cheese
fresh parsley

Preparation time: 15 minutes
Cooking time: 40 minutes

1. Melt the butter in a saucepan, add the onion and fry for about 5 minutes, until softened. Add the rice and stir until all the grains are coated in oil.
2. Add a quarter of the stock, salt and pepper and bring to the boil. Simmer, uncovered, until the stock is absorbed, then gradually add the remaining stock and continue cooking for about 20 minutes, until the rice is tender and the liquid absorbed. Meanwhile make the sauce.
3. Heat the olive oil in a frying pan and fry the garlic and onion for about 5 minutes, until softened and lightly coloured.
4. Add the pepper and chicken livers and cook until the liver turns colour. Stir in the tomato purée, vermouth, water, sage, and add salt and pepper. Simmer uncovered for 10 minutes.
5. Stir the Parmesan cheese into the rice and press into a 20 cm (8 inch) buttered ring mould. Loosen the edges of the mould and invert on to a warm plate.
6. Fill the centre of the mould with sauce. Sprinkle chopped parsley over the rice and arrange sprigs round the outside.

Risotto di gamberoni; Anello di risotto ai fegatini

CALZONE
Fried pizza turnovers

---

1 teaspoon dried yeast
½ teaspoon sugar
50 ml (2 fl oz) warm water
100 g (4 oz) strong plain flour
½ teaspoon salt
1 tablespoon olive oil
oil for deep frying
Filling:
4 thin slices ham
100 g (4 oz) Mozzarella cheese
8 sprigs fresh marjoram or 4 teaspoons dried marjoram
salt
freshly ground black pepper
olive oil

Preparation time: 30 minutes, plus rising
Cooking time: 12-15 minutes

If you wish to cook these turnovers in advance they can be kept warm in the oven for up to 30 minutes without spoiling. Serve two per person for a starter or four each for a main course.

1. Sprinkle the yeast and sugar over the warm water and leave for about 10 minutes until frothy.
2. Place the flour and salt in a bowl. Stir in the oil and the yeast liquid and mix to a soft dough. Knead on a lightly floured surface for about 5 minutes.
3. Place the dough in an oiled polythene bag, loosely tied, and leave in a warm place for about 40 minutes, until doubled in size.
4. Knead the dough briefly until firm. Divide the dough into eight pieces. Roll each piece thinly to a 12 cm (5 inch) round. Place half a slice of ham on each round with a slice of Mozzarella cheese, a sprig of marjoram or ½ teaspoon dried marjoram, salt, pepper and a drizzle of olive oil. Fold the dough over and press the edges to seal. ☐F
5. Heat the oil to 180°C/350°F or until a cube of bread browns in 30 seconds. Fry the calzone, in two or three batches, for 4-5 minutes, until golden brown.
6. Drain on paper towels and serve warm in a folded napkin. As a main course serve with Insalata di bietola e ravanelli (page 67).

☐F Fry from frozen, allowing an extra 2 minutes.

Knead the risen dough until firm.

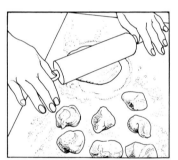
Divide into 8 and roll out thinly.

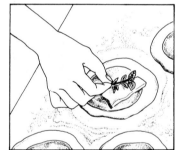
Add the layers of filling.

Fold over and seal the edges.

RISOTTO DI ZUCCHINI
Courgette risotto

---

2 tablespoons olive oil, for frying
1 small onion, peeled and sliced
1 stick celery, chopped
175 g (6 oz) courgettes, thinly sliced
175 g (6 oz) Italian rice
600 ml (1 pint) hot chicken stock
50 g (2 oz) ham, finely chopped
salt
freshly ground black pepper
25 g (1 oz) butter
25 g (1 oz) grated Parmesan cheese

Preparation time: 10 minutes
Cooking time: 25-30 minutes

1. Heat the oil in a saucepan, add the onion and celery and fry gently for 5 minutes. Add the courgettes and cook for a further minute.
2. Add the rice, stirring until all the grains are coated with oil. Add a quarter of the hot stock and bring to the boil. Simmer, uncovered, until the stock is absorbed, then gradually add the remaining stock and continue cooking for about 20 minutes, until the rice is tender and the liquid absorbed.
3. Stir in the ham, salt and pepper and heat through thoroughly. Remove from the heat and quickly stir in the butter and cheese. Serve piping hot on a warmed plate as an accompanying vegetable or starter.

Pinocchiate; Calzone

PINOCCHIATE
Individual pine nut pizzas

3 tablespoons olive oil, for frying
225 g (8 oz) onions, peeled and thinly sliced
1 small red pepper, cored, seeded and sliced
salt
freshly ground black pepper
1 recipe quantity risen dough (see Calzone, page 22)
100 g (4 oz) Bel Paese
50 g (2 oz) stuffed green olives, sliced
25 g (1 oz) pine nuts
2 teaspoons grated Parmesan cheese
2 teaspoons chopped fresh basil or 1 teaspoon dried basil

Preparation time: 20 minutes
Cooking time: 45 minutes
Oven: 200°C, 400°F, Gas Mark 6

1. Heat the oil in a frying pan, add the onions and cook for 5 minutes. Add the red pepper, salt and pepper and cook for a further 5 minutes until the onions are softened and lightly coloured. Cool.
2. Knead the dough briefly on a lightly floured surface. Divide in half and roll out each half to a 20 cm (8 inch) round. Place on a greased baking sheet.
3. Spread the onion mixture evenly over each base. Slice the Bel Paese thinly and arrange over the top. Sprinkle with olives and pine nuts and top with Parmesan cheese. Sprinkle basil over the top. A F
4. Bake in a preheated oven for 35 minutes until the cheese has melted and turned golden brown.

A Store for up to 8 hours in the refrigerator.
F Open freeze, then wrap with freezer film when firm. Cook from frozen on a greased baking sheet, allowing an extra 10 minutes.

PIZZA QUATRO STAGIONI
Four seasons' pizza

1 recipe quantity risen dough (see Calzone page 22)
Tomato sauce:
1 × 225 g (8 oz) can tomatoes
1 teaspoon dried oregano
1 teaspoon sugar
1 tablespoon tomato purée
salt
freshly ground black pepper
100 g (4 oz) Italian Mozzarella cheese, chopped
50 g (2 oz) mushrooms, sliced
2 rashers streaky bacon, chopped
1 × 90 g (3½ oz) can tuna, drained and flaked
1 small green or red pepper, cored, seeded and sliced into
   small lengths
8 black olives

Preparation time: 40 minutes
Cooking time: 35 minutes
Oven: 200°C, 400°F, Gas Mark 6

1. To make the tomato sauce, place the tomatoes in a saucepan with the oregano, sugar, tomato purée, salt and pepper. Bring to the boil, reduce the heat and cook for about 10 minutes, until thickened. Cool. [A]
2. Knead the dough briefly on a lightly floured surface. Cut off a small piece of dough and divide into two.
3. Roll out the large piece of dough to a 22 cm (9 inch) round. Shape each small piece into a 22 cm (9 inch) long sausage. Place these strips across the dough to divide it into four sections.
4. Spread a little of the tomato mixture over each section and sprinkle with chopped Mozzarella cheese.
5. Fill two opposite sections with mushrooms and bacon, then the last two opposite sections with tuna and pepper. [F]
6. Place the olives evenly round the edge of the pizza.
7. Bake in a preheated oven for 35 minutes until the dough is golden and the cheese has melted.

[A] Store the sauce in a covered container in the refrigerator for up to 3 days.
[F] Open freeze, then wrap with freezer film when firm. Cook from frozen, allowing an extra 15 minutes' cooking time.

PIZZA DI CUORE
Heart-shaped pizza

1 × 225 g (8 oz) can tomatoes
2 teaspoons dried oregano
1 garlic clove, peeled and crushed
1 teaspoon sugar
salt
freshly ground black pepper
1 recipe quantity risen dough (see Calzone page 22)
100 g (4 oz) Italian Mozzarella cheese
5 canned artichoke hearts, drained and halved
10 anchovy fillets
1 tablespoon chopped fresh parsley

Preparation time: 35 minutes
Cooking time: 45 minutes
Oven: 200°C, 400°F, Gas Mark 6

1. Place the tomatoes in a saucepan with 1 teaspoon oregano, the garlic, sugar, salt and pepper. Bring to the boil, reduce the heat and cook, uncovered, for about 10 minutes, until thickened. Cool. [A]
2. Knead the dough briefly on a lightly floured surface. Roll out to a 25 cm (10 inch) round. Make an 8 cm (3 inch) cut from the edge towards the centre and tuck under the cut edges to form a heart shape.
3. Place the dough on a greased baking sheet. Spread the tomato sauce evenly over the top. Cut the Mozzarella cheese into 10 slices and place around the edge of the pizza, alternately with the artichoke hearts. Cut each anchovy fillet in half lengthways and place two strips in a cross on each piece of cheese.
4. Sprinkle the remaining oregano and parsley over the top. [F]
5. Bake in a preheated oven for 35 minutes until the dough is golden and the cheese has melted. Serve as a main course with a Green or mixed salad (page 67).

[A] Store the sauce in a covered container in the refrigerator for up to 3 days.
[F] Open freeze, then wrap with freezer film when firm. Cook from frozen, allowing an extra 15 minutes' cooking time.

RISOTTO ALLA POMODORO
Tomato risotto

2 tablespoons olive oil, for frying
1 medium onion, peeled and finely chopped
175 g (6 oz) Italian rice
1 recipe quantity Tomato sauce (page 24)
350 ml (¾ pint) hot stock
salt
freshly ground black pepper

Preparation time: 25 minutes
Cooking time: 30 minutes

1. Heat the oil in a saucepan, add the onion and fry gently for about 5 minutes, until softened. Add the rice and stir until the grains are coated in oil.
2. Add the tomato sauce, a quarter of the stock, salt and pepper. Bring to the boil, then simmer, uncovered, until the stock is absorbed. Gradually add the remaining stock and continue cooking for about 20 minutes, until the rice is tender and all the liquid absorbed.

Variation
Risotto alla romana (Mozzarella and basil risotto).
Omit the tomato sauce and increase the stock to 600 ml (1 pint). Just before serving stir in 2 teaspoons chopped fresh basil and 100 g (4 oz) cubed Italian Mozzarella cheese. Stir gently until the cheese has melted.

RISO AI FUNGHI
Pilaf rice with cèpe mushrooms

---

450 ml (¾ pint) hot chicken stock
½ teaspoon saffron threads
3 tablespoons olive oil
2 shallots, peeled and finely chopped
100 g (4 oz) Italian rice
1 bay leaf
salt
freshly ground black pepper
1 garlic clove, peeled and crushed
100 g (4 oz) cèpe mushrooms, trimmed and sliced
2 tablespoons white wine
To garnish:
2 teaspoons snipped chives

Preparation time: 10 minutes, plus soaking
Cooking time: 35-40 minutes

For a substitute to using cèpe mushrooms see page 9.

1. Pour the hot stock over the saffron threads and leave for about 30 minutes.
2. Heat 2 tablespoons olive oil in a saucepan and fry the shallots for about 5 minutes until softened.
3. Stir in the rice and stir until all the grains are evenly coated with oil. Add the stock together with the saffron threads, bay leaf, salt and pepper. Bring to the boil, reduce the heat, cover and cook gently for 30 minutes, until the rice is tender and the stock absorbed.
4. Meanwhile heat the remaining oil in a small pan, add the garlic and cook for 1 minute. Add the cèpe mushrooms and turn in the oil until coated. Add the wine, salt and pepper and cook gently for 15-20 minutes until the mushrooms are tender.
5. Transfer the rice to a warm serving dish and pour the mushrooms over the top. Sprinkle with chives. Serve as an accompanying vegetable or starter.

SUPPLÌ
Rice croquettes with Mozzarella and ham

2 tablespoons olive oil
1 small onion, peeled and finely chopped
175 g (6 oz) Italian rice, not 'Easy cook'
600 ml (1 pint) hot chicken stock
salt
freshly ground black pepper
50 g (2 oz) Italian Mozzarella cheese
50 g (2 oz) Parma ham
50 g (2 oz) fresh white breadcrumbs
2 teaspoons grated Parmesan cheese
2 teaspoons chopped fresh parsley
oil, for frying

Preparation time: 20 minutes, plus cooling
Cooking time: 45 minutes

1. Heat the olive oil in a saucepan, add the onion and fry for 5 minutes until softened. Add the rice and stir until all the grains are coated with oil.
2. Add a quarter of the hot stock and bring to the boil. Simmer, uncovered, until the stock is absorbed, then gradually add the remaining stock and continue cooking for about 20 minutes, until the rice is tender and the liquid absorbed. Add salt and pepper and leave until the rice is cold.
3. Divide the rice into six equal parts. Divide each part in half and flatten with the hands to form cakes about 8 cm (3 inches) across.
4. Lay a piece of Mozzarella cheese and a piece of Parma ham on one cake and place the other half on top, pressing the edges to seal.
5. Repeat with the remaining mixture to make six croquettes. Mix together the breadcrumbs, Parmesan cheese and parsley. Coat each cake in this mixture.
[A] [F]
6. Heat about 2.5 cm (1 inch) of oil in a frying pan. Fry the croquettes for about 4 minutes on each side, until golden brown and crispy.
7. Drain on paper towels and serve hot.

[A] Store in the refrigerator for up to 24 hours.
[F] Cook from frozen, allowing 5-6 minutes each side.

Riso ai funghi; Supplì

LASAGNE
Veal and bacon lasagne

2 tablespoons olive oil, for frying
1 small onion, peeled and chopped
1 garlic clove, peeled and crushed
2 rashers streaky bacon, rinded and diced
350 g (12 oz) minced veal
2 teaspoons chopped fresh sage or 1 teaspoon dried sage
1 tomato, skinned and chopped
120 ml (4 fl oz) white wine
salt
freshly ground black pepper
25 g (1 oz) grated Parmesan cheese
100 g (4 oz) lasagne
Béchamel sauce:
25 g (1 oz) butter
25 g (1 oz) plain flour
300 ml (½ pint) milk
150 ml (¼ pint) single cream
pinch of nutmeg

Preparation time: 35 minutes
Cooking time: about 1 hour
Oven: 200°C, 400°F, Gas Mark 6

Minced veal is available from some supermarkets, butchers and freezer centres. If it is difficult to find you can buy pie veal and mince it yourself.

1. Heat the oil in a saucepan and fry the onion, garlic and bacon for about 5 minutes. Add the minced veal and fry until lightly browned.
2. Add the sage, tomato, wine, salt and pepper. Bring to the boil, reduce the heat and cook gently, uncovered, for 20 minutes, until the veal is tender.
3. To make the Béchamel sauce, heat the butter in a saucepan, add the flour and cook for 1 minute. Gradually stir in the milk, cooking until thickened and smooth. Stir in the cream and nutmeg. Add salt and pepper and cook for 2 minutes.
4. Spread a little sauce in the base of a buttered shallow oblong dish. Sprinkle with a little Parmesan cheese and cover with one-third of the lasagne, taking care not to overlap the pieces.
5. Spread one-third of the remaining sauce evenly over the lasagne. Sprinkle with cheese. Spoon over one-third of the meat mixture. Cover with lasagne.
6. Repeat these layers twice more, finishing with meat mixture and cheese. [A] [F]
7. Bake in a preheated oven for 35 minutes until the lasagne is cooked and the topping is golden.

[A] Store in the refrigerator for up to 24 hours before cooking.
[F] Cook from frozen, allowing an extra 15-20 minutes' cooking time.

FETTUCINE CON POLLO
Noodles with chicken and tomatoes

---

1 tablespoon olive oil, for frying
100 g (4 oz) boneless chicken breast, chopped
1 small onion, peeled and chopped
1 stick celery, chopped
1 carrot, peeled and chopped
1 teaspoon dried oregano
4 tablespoons red wine
1 × 225 g (8 oz) can tomatoes
salt
freshly ground black pepper
175 g (6 oz) fettucine or tagliatelle
To garnish:
celery leaves

Preparation time: 10 minutes
Cooking time: 20 minutes

1. Heat the olive oil in a saucepan and fry the chicken until lightly coloured. Add the onion, celery and carrot and cook for 5 minutes until softened.
2. Add the oregano, wine, tomatoes, salt and pepper. Bring to the boil, reduce the heat, cover and cook for 10 minutes.
3. Meanwhile cook the fettucine in plenty of boiling salted water for 4-5 minutes for fresh pasta or 7-8 minutes for dried (or follow directions on the pack) until just cooked or 'al dente'.
4. Drain well and mix with the chicken sauce. Transfer to a warm serving dish and garnish with celery leaves.

SPAGHETTI ALLA MARINARA
Seafood spaghetti

---

2 tablespoons olive oil
2 garlic cloves, peeled and crushed
100 g (4 oz) frozen mussels, thawed
100 g (4 oz) peeled prawns
4 tablespoons white wine
salt
freshly ground black pepper
150 ml (¼ pint) double cream
pinch cayenne pepper
165 g (6 oz) spaghetti
1 tablespoon chopped fresh parsley
To garnish:
4 unpeeled prawns
quartered lemon slices

Preparation time: 10 minutes
Cooking time: 15 minutes

FARFALLE AL MASCARPONE E NOCE
Pasta bows in walnut cheese sauce

---

175 g (6 oz) pasta bows
100 g (4 oz) curd cheese
150 ml (¼ pint) single cream
1 tablespoon grated Parmesan cheese
salt
freshly ground black pepper
1-2 tablespoons milk (optional)
1 tablespoon olive oil
1 teaspoon lemon juice
To garnish:
25 g (1 oz) walnuts, roughly chopped
2 teaspoons snipped chives

Preparation time: 5 minutes
Cooking time: 12-15 minutes

Use 100 g (4 oz) pasta for a starter, or serve with Insalata di fagiolini (page 67) for a main course.

1. Cook the pasta bows in plenty of boiling salted water for 6-8 minutes (or follow directions on the pack) until just cooked or 'al dente'. Meanwhile make the sauce.
2. Gently heat the curd cheese until it forms a thick sauce. Stir in the cream, Parmesan cheese, salt and pepper. Heat, stirring, until smooth and creamy. If it seems a little thick add 1-2 tablespoons milk.
3. Drain the pasta and mix with the oil and lemon juice. Divide between two dishes. Pour over the sauce and sprinkle with walnuts and chives.

If you are able to buy fresh mussels, cook them as follows: scrub 225 g (8 oz) mussels and remove the beards, discarding any that are open. Place in a heavy pan over a medium heat and cover tightly. Shake the pan until the shells open. Remove from the heat and drain. Discard the shells.

1. Heat 1 tablespoon oil in a saucepan, add the garlic and fry gently for 1 minute. Add the mussels, prawns, white wine, salt and pepper. Cook for a further 3 minutes.
2. Stir in the cream and cayenne and heat through.
3. Meanwhile cook the spaghetti in plenty of boiling salted water for 8-10 minutes (or follow directions on the pack) until just cooked or 'al dente'.
4. Drain the spaghetti and mix with the remaining olive oil and the parsley. Serve with the seafood sauce and garnished with whole prawns and lemon.

TOP TO BOTTOM: Fettucine con pollo; Farfalle al mascarpone e noce; Spaghetti alla marinara

Macaroni alla romagnola; Cannelloni piacentini

MACARONI ALLA ROMAGNOLA
Macaroni with sausage and tomato sauce

225 g (8 oz) Italian sausages
1 tablespoon olive oil, for frying
1 garlic clove, peeled and crushed
1 small onion, peeled and roughly chopped
1 small red pepper, cored, seeded and cut into cubes
350 g (12 oz) tomatoes, skinned and chopped
1 teaspoon dried oregano
1 tablespoon tomato purée
3 tablespoons Marsala or sherry
salt
freshly ground black pepper
100 g (4 oz) macaroni
15 g (½ oz) butter

Preparation time: 20 minutes
Cooking time: 20 minutes

Many delicatessens and supermarkets now sell Italian sausages, called Salsicce (see page 8). To serve this as a starter you could omit the sausage and simply sprinkle the tomato sauce with grated Parmesan.

1. Skin the sausages and break each one into 4-5 pieces. Heat the oil in a saucepan. Add the garlic and onion and fry until softened and lightly coloured.
2. Add the sausage to the pan and fry until evenly browned. Add the red pepper, tomatoes, oregano, tomato purée, Marsala or sherry, salt and pepper. Cook gently, uncovered, for 12-15 minutes. [A]
3. Meanwhile boil the macaroni in plenty of boiling salted water for 8-10 minutes, or follow the directions on the pack, until just cooked or 'al dente'. Drain well and stir in the butter.
4. Mix together the pasta and sauce and transfer to a warm serving dish or two individual dishes.

[A] The sauce can be made up to 24 hours in advance and reheated while the macaroni is cooking.

CANNELLONI PIACENTINI
Ricotta and spinach cannelloni

225 g (8 oz) spinach, washed
100 g (4 oz) ricotta cheese
1 tablespoon grated Parmesan cheese
2 pinches grated nutmeg
1 egg yolk
1 tablespoon chopped fresh mixed herbs, i.e. marjoram, chives, parsley, chervil
salt
freshly ground black pepper
100 g (4 oz) cannelloni
2 tablespoons grated Parmesan cheese, for sprinkling
Tomato sauce:
450 g (1 lb) ripe tomatoes, skinned and chopped
1 small onion, peeled and chopped
1 stick celery, chopped
1 tablespoon tomato purée
½ teaspoon sugar
salt
freshly ground black pepper

Preparation time: 30 minutes
Cooking time: about 1 hour
Oven: 180°C, 350°F, Gas Mark 4

Most cannelloni you buy now is precooked and need not be boiled before baking. If you find ricotta cheese unobtainable, drained and sieved cottage cheese or curd cheese can be used instead.

1. Place the spinach in a saucepan with just the water that clings to it. Cover and cook for 7-10 minutes, shaking the pan occasionally, until the spinach is tender. Drain well and chop finely.
2. Place the spinach in a bowl with the ricotta cheese, Parmesan cheese, nutmeg, egg yolk, herbs, salt and pepper. Mix well.
3. Carefully fill the cannelloni tubes with the spinach mixture, using a small teaspoon. Place in a buttered shallow ovenproof dish in one layer.
4. Place all the sauce ingredients in a saucepan, bring to the boil, reduce the heat and cook, uncovered, for 20 minutes. Press through a sieve or liquidize until fairly smooth.
5. Pour the tomato sauce evenly over the cannelloni, ensuring they are all covered. Sprinkle with Parmesan cheese. A F
6. Bake, uncovered, in a preheated oven for 35-40 minutes, until the cannelloni are tender. (Test by piercing with a sharp pointed knife.)

A Can be made up to 24 hours in advance and stored in the refrigerator until ready to cook.
F Cook, uncovered, from frozen, allowing an extra 15-20 minutes.

TAGLIATELLE VERDI ALLA GHIOTTA
Green noodles with cream, ham and mushrooms

40 g (1½ oz) butter
2 shallots or small onions, peeled and finely chopped
100 g (4 oz) ham, diced
100 g (4 oz) button mushrooms, sliced
150 ml (¼ pint) double cream
1 tablespoon chopped fresh parsley
1 tablespoon grated Parmesan cheese
salt
freshly ground black pepper
150 g (6 oz) tagliatelle verde

Preparation time: 10 minutes
Cooking time: 15 minutes

This dish is very quick to cook. Have your ingredients ready prepared and measured and all that's left is the final assembly. If possible, use fresh or frozen pasta for this dish.

1. Heat 25 g (1 oz) of the butter in a frying pan. Add the shallots and cook for about 3 minutes, until softened. Add the ham and mushrooms and cook for a further 2 minutes.
2. Stir in the cream, parsley, 2 teaspoons Parmesan cheese, salt and pepper. Lower the heat and cook for 5 minutes.
3. Meanwhile, using a large pan cook the pasta in plenty of boiling salted water for 4-5 minutes for fresh pasta or 7-8 minutes for dried (or follow directions on the pack) until just cooked or 'al dente'. Drain well and stir in the remaining butter and Parmesan cheese.
4. Place the tagliatelle on a warmed serving dish and make a depression in the centre. Pour in the creamy sauce and serve at once.

To serve pasta as an accompaniment to a main meal there are several delicious ways to make it taste extra special. Cook it as described on page 9, then stir in any one of the following, just before serving. (Make sure though that your serving dish is warmed, otherwise the pasta will quickly cool and become less appetizing.)
1. 25 g (1 oz) butter, 1 teaspoon chopped fresh parsley, marjoram or tarragon, and 1 tablespoon lemon juice.
2. 25 g (1 oz) butter and 1 tablespoon pine nuts.
3. 1 tablespoon Pesto (page 13).
4. 1 tablespoon grated Parmesan cheese and 25 g (1 oz) butter.
5. ½ recipe quantity Tomato sauce (page 24).

FISH

SCAMPI AGLI STECCHI
Marinated scampi skewers

225 g (8 oz) scampi
Marinade:
2 garlic cloves, peeled and crushed
3 tablespoons olive oil
2 tablespoons chopped fresh parsley
2 teaspoons lemon juice
1 tablespoon dry white breadcrumbs
salt
freshly ground black pepper
bay leaves

Preparation time: 10 minutes, plus marinating
Cooking time: 5-8 minutes

1. Rinse the scampi and dry well with paper towels.
2. Mix together the garlic, oil, parsley, lemon juice, breadcrumbs, salt and pepper. Add the scampi and mix well. Leave to marinate for a minimum of 1 hour. [A]
3. Thread the scampi on to 4 skewers, placing an occasional bay leaf between. Place under a preheated moderate grill, turning occasionally until golden and crispy.
4. Riso ai funghi (page 26) and a crisp green salad or Insalata di radicchio (page 65) make good accompaniments.
5. Serve with a dry white wine or a light red wine.

[A] Marinate the fish overnight.

Marinating whole fish such as plaice, sole, or trout, adds a special flavour and succulence. For the marinade mix together: 4 tablespoons olive oil, 1 tablespoon lemon juice, 2 teaspoons chopped fresh herbs (i.e. rosemary, chives, or mint) salt and freshly ground black pepper.
Take the cleaned fish and using a sharp knife make 3 diagonal cuts across the flesh. Pour the marinade over. Cover and refrigerate for at least 2-12 hours (the longer the better). Grill the fish, basting occasionally with the marinade. The cooking time will be about 8-10 minutes for plaice or sole, and about 12-15 minutes for trout, depending on thickness and size.

SALMONE CON SALSA PICCANTE
Salmon with caper and parsley sauce

2 × 225 g (8 oz) salmon steaks
salt
freshly ground black pepper
Poaching liquid:
150 ml (¼ pint) dry white wine
1 bay leaf
3 sprigs parsley
1 shallot or small onion, peeled and chopped
few celery leaves
Sauce:
25 g (1 oz) butter
1 garlic clove, peeled and crushed
1 tablespoon capers, drained and chopped
2 tablespoons chopped fresh parsley
To garnish:
celery leaves

Preparation time: 10 minutes
Cooking time: 25 minutes

1. Wipe the salmon steaks and sprinkle on both sides with salt and pepper.
2. Place all the poaching ingredients in a shallow pan and bring to a gentle simmer. Add the salmon steaks and cover the pan. Cook on a low heat for 12-15 minutes until the fish is cooked.
3. Remove the salmon from the liquid and place on a warmed serving plate. Keep warm while preparing the sauce. Strain the liquid and reserve.
4. Melt the butter in a small pan, add the garlic, capers and parsley and cook for 1 minute. Add salt, pepper and 4 tablespoons of the poaching liquid.
5. Bring to the boil and pour over the salmon. Garnish with celery leaves.
6. Serve with a light dry white wine.

Salmone con salsa piccante; Scampi agli stecchi

PESCE IN GRATICOLA
Halibut with raisins and olives

2 small halibut steaks, or 1 large steak, halved
seasoned flour
2 tablespoons olive oil, for frying
1 garlic clove, peeled and crushed
1 small onion, peeled and chopped
1 stick celery, chopped
25 g (1 oz) seedless raisins
50 g (2 oz) stoned olives
4 tablespoons white wine
salt
freshly ground black pepper
To garnish:
celery leaves

Preparation time: 10 minutes
Cooking time: about 20 minutes

1. Wash the halibut and pat dry with paper towels. Toss in seasoned flour.
2. Heat the oil in a frying pan. Fry the fish for 10-12 minutes, until golden brown and cooked through, turning once.
3. Remove the fish from the pan with a fish slice and place on a serving plate. Keep warm.
4. Add the garlic, onion and celery to the pan and fry for about 5 minutes, until softened. Add the raisins, olives, wine, salt and pepper. Cook for a further 5 minutes.
5. Pour the sauce over the fish and garnish with celery leaves. Fried or steamed potatoes make a good accompaniment.
6. Serve with a dry white wine.

TROTA IN CARTOCCIO
Baked trout parcels

2 × 350 g (12 oz) trout, cleaned
salt
freshly ground black pepper
2 tablespoons olive oil
2 garlic cloves, peeled and crushed
1 medium onion, peeled and chopped
1 stick celery, chopped
4 sprigs rosemary
2 tablespoons white wine
To garnish:
sprigs of rosemary

Preparation time: 10 minutes
Cooking time: 30 minutes
Oven: 180°C, 350°F, Gas Mark 4

1. Wash the trout and dry well with paper towels. Sprinkle inside and out with salt and pepper.
2. Heat the olive oil in a frying pan, add the garlic, onion and celery and fry gently for 5 minutes until softened. Add salt and pepper, 2 sprigs rosemary and the wine and cook for a further 5 minutes.
3. Brush with oil two double sheets of greaseproof paper large enough to enclose the fish. Divide the filling between the pieces of paper and place the trout on top. Place a sprig of rosemary on each fish.
4. Wrap the fish loosely to enclose it and place on a baking sheet. Bake in a preheated oven for 20 minutes until the fish is tender.

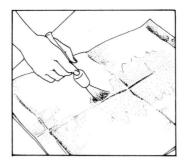
Brush the double sheets of greaseproof paper with oil.

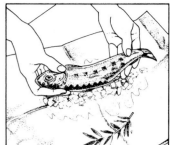
Divide the filling between the two sheets and put the trout on top.

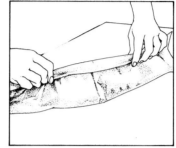
Secure the sides with a double fold.

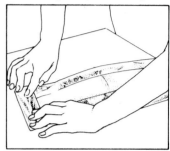
Double fold the ends.

5. Remove the fish from the paper and serve garnished with sprigs of rosemary.
6. Serve with a fruity dry white wine.

Variation
Trout can be replaced by mullet, mackerel, or salmon steaks.

SPIGOLA ALLA MENTA
Sea bass baked with mint

1 × 750 g (1½ lb) sea bass, cleaned and scaled
salt
freshly ground black pepper
olive oil, for brushing
150 ml (¼ pint) dry white wine
Stuffing:
bunch of mint leaves
25 g (1 oz) softened butter
50 g (2 oz) white breadcrumbs
2 tablespoons lemon juice
salt
freshly ground black pepper
To serve:
bed of mint leaves
quartered lemon slices

Pesce con uva passa; Spigola alla menta

Preparation time: 20 minutes
Cooking time: 40-45 minutes
Oven: 180°C, 350°F, Gas Mark 4

If sea bass is not available, grey mullet or hake can be used instead. Soak grey mullet overnight in salted water before cooking.

1. Wash the sea bass and dry with paper towels. Sprinkle inside and out with salt and pepper.
2. Chop 2 tablespoons mint leaves and mix with the butter, breadcrumbs, lemon juice, salt and pepper. Stuff the fish cavity with this mixture.
3. Place the fish in a baking dish and brush with olive oil. Arrange mint leaves, overlapping, to cover the fish. Pour on the wine and cover with foil.
4. Bake in a preheated oven for 40-45 minutes until the fish is tender. Arrange on a bed of mint leaves and a line of lemon slices down the centre. Asparagi all'Italiana or Sformato di piselli makes a good accompaniment (page 56).
5. Serve with a dry white wine.

CALAMARI IN UMIDO
Squid in red wine

225 g (8 oz) squid, prepared
2 tablespoons lemon juice
3 tablespoons olive oil
1 large onion, peeled and sliced into rings
2 garlic cloves, peeled and crushed
2 tomatoes, skinned and chopped
sprig of thyme and marjoram
200 ml (8 fl oz) red wine
1 tablespoon tomato purée
salt
freshly ground black pepper
To garnish:
sprigs of thyme or marjoram
lemon wedges

Preparation time: 15 minutes, plus marinating
Cooking time: 1½ hours
Oven: 160°C, 325°F, Gas Mark 3

Your fishmonger will prepare the squid, or buy frozen which is ready prepared. Squid lends itself well to a rich, strong sauce such as this one.

1. Slice the squid thinly into rings. Place in a bowl with the lemon juice and marinate for 1 hour.
2. Heat the oil in a flameproof casserole, add the onion and garlic and fry for about 5 minutes. Add the squid and cook for a further 2 minutes.
3. Add the tomatoes, herbs, wine, tomato purée, salt and pepper. Mix well and bring to the boil.
4. Cover the casserole and cook in a preheated oven for 1¼ hours until the squid is tender. Garnish with the sprigs of thyme or marjoram and lemon wedges. Polenta con formaggio (page 59) or Risotto di zucchini (page 22) make good accompaniments.
5. Serve with a robust red wine.

Zuppa di pesce, with toasted French bread; Calamari in umido; Frittura di scampi alla maionese verde

ZUPPA DI PESCE
Seafood casserole

2 tablespoons olive oil
1 garlic clove, peeled and crushed
1 medium onion, peeled and chopped
1 small red pepper, cored, seeded and chopped
450 g (1 lb) mixed seafood, such as red mullet, scampi, prawns, cod, hake, sole, cut into pieces or steaks
2 tomatoes, skinned and sliced
150 ml (¼ pint) white wine
50 g (2 oz) whole button mushrooms
salt
freshly ground black pepper
To serve:
toasted French bread

Preparation time: 10 minutes
Cooking time: 20-25 minutes

Choose 2 or 3 types of fish for this recipe, including in your choice one firm white fish and one shell-fish.

1. Heat the oil in a medium saucepan, add the garlic and onion and fry gently for about 5 minutes.
2. Add the red pepper and cook for 2 minutes. Add the fish and stir to coat in oil.
3. Add the tomatoes, wine, mushrooms, salt and pepper. Bring to the boil, then simmer uncovered for 15-20 minutes until the fish is tender. Serve with toasted French bread and a salad.
4. Serve a light dry white wine or a light red wine.

FRITTURA DI SCAMPI ALLA MAIONESE VERDE
King prawn fritters with green mayonnaise

8 king prawns, peeled
1 tablespoon lemon juice
salt
freshly ground black pepper
oil, for deep frying
Green mayonnaise:
150 ml (¼ pint) mayonnaise
3 tablespoons chopped fresh parsley
2 teaspoons chopped fresh basil
1 tablespoon pine nuts, finely chopped
1 tablespoon pistachio nuts, chopped
1 garlic clove, peeled and crushed (optional)
salt
freshly ground black pepper
Batter:
50 g (2 oz) plain flour
2 tablespoons olive oil
4 tablespoons water
1 egg white (size 4, 5)

Preparation time: 20 minutes
Cooking time: 5 minutes

1. Place the prawns in a bowl and sprinkle over lemon juice, salt and pepper.
2. Mix together all the green mayonnaise ingredients until thoroughly blended. **A**
3. Make the batter. Place the flour in a bowl with a good shake of salt and pepper. Add the oil and water and mix to form a smooth batter.
4. Whisk the egg white until it forms soft peaks. Fold into the batter, using a metal spoon, taking care not to knock out the air.
5. Heat the oil to 180°C/350°F or until a cube of bread browns in 30 seconds. Dip the prawns in the batter and deep fry for about 5 minutes until golden.
6. Drain well on paper towels and serve with the mayonnaise separately.
7. Serve with a dry white wine.

A The prawns and mayonnaise can be prepared up to 24 hours in advance and stored separately in the refrigerator.

TRIGLIE ALLA GRIGLIA
Red mullet with tomato and anchovy

3 tablespoons olive oil
1 garlic clove, peeled and crushed
1 × 225 g (8 oz) can tomatoes
3 anchovy fillets, chopped
2 tablespoons chopped fresh parsley
pinch of sugar
freshly ground black pepper
2 red mullet, about 450 g (1lb) in weight each, cleaned
salt
To garnish:
2 anchovy fillets, halved lengthways
sprigs of Continental parsley

Preparation time: 20 minutes
Cooking time: 20-25 minutes

1. First make the sauce. Heat 2 tablespoons olive oil in a saucepan. Add the garlic and fry gently until lightly coloured. Add the tomatoes, chopped anchovies, parsley, sugar and pepper. Bring to the boil, then simmer, uncovered, for 20-25 minutes, until thickened. ⒜
2. Meanwhile cook the mullet. Sprinkle the fish inside and out with salt and pepper. Brush the skin with the remaining olive oil. Make two diagonal slits in each side of the fish.
3. Place the fish under a preheated moderate grill for 7 minutes each side. Place on a warmed serving dish and pour some of the sauce over the centre. Serve the remaining sauce separately. Garnish with strips of anchovy and Continental parsley. Carciofi fritti (page 61) makes a good accompaniment.
4. Serve with a light red wine.

⒜ Make the sauce up to 24 hours in advance and store in a covered container in the refrigerator.

Red mullet is an oily fish with a firm white flesh. It is available fresh from May through to September and is also sold frozen. To scale and cut a mullet, hold the fish firmly by the tail with paper towels. Scrape down from the tail towards the head using the back of a knife. Do this in the sink or on newspaper to catch the scales and spiky fins. Next, cut down the belly from the head to the vent, remove the entrails and run the point of the knife down either side of the backbone to remove the blood vessels. Scrape out any black skin. Wash the mullet thoroughly under running cold water and dry on paper towels, ready for cooking.

Trota marinata all'arancia; Sogliole alla veneziana; Sarde ripiene

TROTA MARINATA ALL'ARANCIA
Orange-marinated cold trout

2 × 350 g (12 oz) trout, cleaned
seasoned flour
4 tablespoons olive oil, for frying
Marinade:
2 oranges
1 lemon
1 small onion, peeled and finely chopped
150 ml (¼ pint) dry white wine
2 bay leaves
salt
freshly ground black pepper
To garnish:
quartered orange slices

Preparation time: 15 minutes, plus soaking and marinating
Cooking time: 17-20 minutes

1. Wash the trout and pat dry with paper towels. Toss in seasoned flour.
2. Heat 3 tablespoons oil in a large frying pan. Add the trout and cook for 12-15 minutes, turning once. Remove from the heat and drain on paper towels. When cold place on a serving dish.
3. Pare the rind from half an orange and half a lemon, taking care not to include any white pith. Cut into thin matchstick-sized strips. Place in a bowl, pour over boiling water and soak for 20 minutes. Squeeze the juice from the oranges and lemon.
4. Heat the remaining oil in a small pan, add the onion and fry for about 5 minutes, until softened. Drain the orange and lemon strips, discard the liquid, and add the strips to the pan with the orange and lemon juice, wine, bay leaves, salt and pepper.
5. Pour over the fish and leave to marinate for at least 6 hours or overnight in the refrigerator. [A]
6. Garnish the fish with orange slices.
7. Serve with a fruity dry white wine.

[A] Leave to marinate for up to 24 hours.

SARDE RIPIENE
Stuffed sardines

350 g (12 oz) sardines, cleaned
salt
freshly ground black pepper
Stuffing:
4 tablespoons chopped fresh parsley
50 g (2 oz) breadcrumbs
1 tablespoon lemon juice
1 tablespoon grated Parmesan cheese
25 g (1 oz) melted butter
salt
freshly ground black pepper
To garnish:
Continental parsley
lemon wedges

Preparation time: 10 minutes
Cooking time: 6-8 minutes

1. Wash the sardines and pat dry with paper towels. Sprinkle well with salt and pepper.
2. Mix together the parsley, breadcrumbs, lemon juice, Parmesan cheese, butter, salt and pepper. **A**
3. Fill the cavity of each fish with a little stuffing.
4. Place the sardines under a preheated hot grill for 6-8 minutes, turning once. Tiny chips and Insalata di radicchio (page 65) make good accompaniments.
5. Serve a light dry white wine or light red wine.

A Make the stuffing the previous day, but do not stuff the fish.

SOGLIOLE ALLA VENEZIANA
Venetian-style sole

2 Dover sole, cleaned and skinned on dark side
Savoury butter:
50 g (2 oz) softened butter
2 teaspoons chopped fresh mint
2 teaspoons chopped fresh parsley
1 garlic clove, peeled and crushed
salt
freshly ground black pepper
Sauce:
25 g (1 oz) butter
1 shallot, peeled and finely chopped
120 ml (4 fl oz) white wine
4 tablespoons double cream
To garnish:
sprig of parsley

Preparation time: 20 minutes
Cooking time: about 15 minutes

1. Wash the fish and pat dry with paper towels. Using a sharp knife, make two or three diagonal slits in each side of the flesh.
2. Blend together all the savoury butter ingredients and spread a quarter over one side of each fish.
3. Next make the sauce. Melt the butter in a small pan, add the shallot and cook gently for about 5 minutes until softened. Stir in the wine with salt and pepper and cook for a further 2 minutes. Keep warm while cooking the fish.
4. Place the fish, butter side up, under a preheated moderate grill and cook for 3-4 minutes. Turn the fish over and spread with the remaining butter. Cook for a further 3 minutes.
5. Stir the cream into the sauce and bring briefly to the boil. Place the fish on a warmed serving plate, pour over a little sauce, and garnish with parsley. Serve the remaining sauce separately.
6. Serve with a dry white wine.

MEAT & POULTRY

VITELLO TONNATO
Veal with tuna mayonnaise

450 g (1 lb) boned leg of veal
1 medium onion, peeled and quartered
2 cloves
1 bay leaf
1 stick celery, chopped
1 carrot, peeled and chopped
4 peppercorns
Tuna mayonnaise:
1 × 90 g (3½ oz) can tuna fish, drained
1 egg yolk
2 anchovy fillets, finely chopped
1 tablespoon lemon juice
1 tablespoon capers
salt
freshly ground black pepper
85 ml (3 fl oz) olive oil
To garnish:
anchovy fillets
capers
lemon slices

Preparation time: 30 minutes, plus cooling and marinating
Cooking time: 1 hour

1. Tie the veal into a neat shape with string. Place in a saucepan with the onion, cloves, bay leaf, celery, carrot and peppercorns and water to cover.
2. Bring to the boil and skim off any scum. Reduce the heat, cover and simmer for 1 hour until the veal is tender. Leave the meat to cool in the stock. [F]
3. Mash the tuna finely with a fork. Blend the egg yolk with the anchovies, lemon juice, capers and a little salt and pepper using a liquidizer or food processor.
4. While the machine is running pour in the olive oil in a fine steady stream. Continue until all the oil is added and the mayonnaise is thick and creamy.
5. Add the tuna and blend until smooth. Taste and adjust the seasoning. If the mayonnaise seems a little too thick add a spoonful of the stock and blend.
6. Remove the cold veal from the stock, cut into thin slices and arrange on a serving dish. Spread the sauce over the top to enclose the meat completely.
7. Cover the dish with foil or cling film and leave in the refrigerator for at least 8 hours or overnight.
8. Arrange a lattice of anchovy over the tuna, placing capers in between. Garnish with lemon.
9. Serve with a light dry white wine.

[F] Freeze meat and stock separately. Thaw the meat slowly in the refrigerator and proceed from step 3. The unused stock is good for soups and casseroles.

PERNICI RIPIENE
Stuffed partridges

2 partridges, with their livers
salt
freshly ground black pepper
50 g (2 oz) mushrooms, finely chopped
175 g (6 oz) unsmoked streaky bacon rashers
3 juniper berries, crushed
25 g (1 oz) butter
2 slices bread, cut into rounds
To garnish:
watercress

Preparation time: 20 minutes
Cooking time: 40-45 minutes
Oven: 200°C, 400°F, Gas Mark 6

1. Wash the partridges and dry well with paper towels. Sprinkle with salt and pepper.
2. Chop the partridge liver finely and mix with the mushrooms. Reserve 4 slices of bacon and rind and chop the remainder. Mix with the mushrooms and liver, adding the juniper berries, salt and pepper.
3. Stuff the birds and wrap 2 slices of bacon around each. Place in a small roasting tin with the butter.
4. Roast in a preheated oven for 35-40 minutes until the birds are tender. Remove and keep warm.
5. Heat the pan juices on top of the stove. Fry the bread in the juices until crisp and golden, then place on a warmed dish with the partridges on top, and garnish with watercress. Fave alla Mortadella (page 62) and Gnocchi di patate (page 58), or Polenta con formaggio (page 59) make good accompaniments.
6. Serve with a robust red wine.

Vitello tonnato; Pernici ripiene

BISTECCHINE CASANOVA
Marsala steaks with brandy

2 rump or sirloin steaks, about 225 g (8 oz) each
salt
freshly ground black pepper
25 g (1 oz) butter
2 teaspoons olive oil
50 g (2 oz) mushrooms, finely chopped
25 g (1 oz) smooth pâté
2 tablespoons Marsala
3 tablespoons brandy
To garnish:
sprig of lemon, thyme or parsley

Preparation time: 10 minutes
Cooking time: 10-15 minutes

1. Sprinkle the steaks on both sides with salt and pepper.
2. Heat the butter and oil in a frying pan. When foaming add the steaks and fry for 2-4 minutes on each side until browned and cooked to your liking. Transfer to a warm dish and keep warm.
3. Add the mushrooms to the pan and cook on a high heat for 1 minute, stirring continuously. Add the pâté and Marsala and stir until well mixed and hot. Sprinkle with salt and pepper. Spread the mixture over the steaks and return them to the frying pan.
4. Warm the brandy and pour over the steaks, at the table. Carefully ignite the brandy and serve when the flames have extinguished. Garnish with a sprig of thyme or parsley.
5. Serve with a dry red or robust red wine.

POLPETTONE ALLA TOSCANA
Beef roll with mushroom sauce

225 g (8 oz) lean minced beef
salt
freshly ground black pepper
50 g (2 oz) fresh white breadcrumbs
1 small onion, peeled and finely chopped
50 g (2 oz) unsmoked bacon, rinded and finely chopped
1 tablespoon grated Parmesan cheese
1 garlic clove, peeled and crushed
1 egg, beaten
1 tablespoon olive oil
Sauce:
1 tablespoon tomato purée
120 ml (4 fl oz) red wine
120 ml (4 fl oz) water
100 g (4 oz) mushrooms, sliced

Preparation time: 25 minutes, plus chilling
Cooking time: 45 minutes

1. Place the minced beef in a large bowl with a good shake of salt and pepper. Add half the breadcrumbs, with the onion, bacon, Parmesan cheese, garlic and egg.
2. Mix with a fork or the hands until all the ingredients are well blended.
3. Shape the meat mixture into a short roll about 7.5 cm (3 inches) in diameter. Roll in the remaining breadcrumbs and chill for 30 minutes. [A]
4. Heat the oil in a large, heavy saucepan, add the meat roll and fry for about 5 minutes, turning until evenly browned.
5. Mix together the tomato purée, wine, water, salt and pepper. Pour around the meat roll and bring to the boil. Lower the heat, cover and simmer for 30 minutes.
6. Add the mushrooms to the sauce and cook for a further 10 minutes. [F]
7. Remove the roll from the pan and cut into thin slices. Pour some of the sauce into a serving dish and arrange the meat slices in a row over the top. Serve any remaining sauce separately. Fave alla Mortadella (page 62) and Gnocchi di patate (page 58) or Polenta con formaggio (page 59) make good accompaniments.
8. Serve with a robust red wine.

[A] Store the uncooked roll for up to 24 hours in the refrigerator.
[F] Thaw overnight in the refrigerator. Simmer in a covered pan for 10-15 minutes until heated through, then proceed with step 7.

INVOLTINI ALLA BARESE
Beef olives

4 thin slices leg of mutton cut of beef
2 teaspoons chopped fresh parsley
2 teaspoons chopped fresh basil or 1 teaspoon dried basil
1 tablespoon grated Parmesan cheese
1 garlic clove, peeled and crushed
salt
freshly ground black pepper
4 thin slices of ham
2 tablespoons olive oil
1 small onion, peeled and sliced
50 ml (2 fl oz) red wine
50 ml (2 fl oz) beef stock or water
2 tomatoes, skinned and chopped
To garnish:
parsley sprigs or basil leaves

Preparation time: 20 minutes
Cooking time: 1 hour 10 minutes

If you are unable to obtain leg of mutton cut of beef from your butcher, use thin slices of topside instead.

1. Place the slices of meat between two sheets of greaseproof paper and flatten with a rolling pin, or ask your butcher to do this.
2. Mix together the parsley, basil, Parmesan cheese and garlic.
3. Sprinkle the slices of meat with salt and pepper and cover each with a slice of ham, trimming to fit if necessary.
4. Put a little herb mixture at one end of each slice. Sprinkle with a little salt and pepper. Roll up the slices, securing with cotton or fine string. [A]
5. Heat the oil in a large saucepan, add the onion and fry for about 5 minutes, until softened and slightly browned. Add the beef olives and fry for a further 5 minutes until evenly browned.
6. Add to the pan the wine, stock, tomatoes and a little salt and pepper. Bring to the boil, cover and simmer for 1 hour until the beef is tender. [F]
7. Remove the beef rolls from the sauce and remove the string or cotton. Place on a warmed serving platter. Pour over the sauce and garnish with parsley or basil. Frittura di carciofi di giudea (page 61) makes a good accompaniment.
8. Serve with a dry red wine.

[A] Store the uncooked rolls for up to 12 hours in the refrigerator.
[F] Thaw the rolls overnight in the refrigerator and simmer in a covered pan for 10-15 minutes until heated through.

Bistecchine casanova; Polpettone alla toscana

ARROSTO DI AGNELLO AL GINEPRO
Marinated pot roasted lamb

Half a small leg or shoulder of lamb, about 750 g (1½ lb)
1 stick celery, chopped
1 carrot, peeled and chopped
1 onion, peeled and chopped
6 juniper berries, bruised
300 ml (½ pint) red wine
3 sprigs rosemary or ½ teaspoon dried rosemary
2 garlic cloves, peeled
1 tablespoon olive oil, for frying
salt
freshly ground black pepper
1 tablespoon redcurrant jelly

Preparation time: 25 minutes, plus marinating
Cooking time: 1¾ hours

1. Place the lamb in a large bowl with the celery, carrot, onion, juniper berries, wine, rosemary and garlic. Cover and marinate for up to 24 hours, turning occasionally.

Shoulder of lamb is less expensive and has a sweeter flavour than leg, although it does tend to be marbled with more fat. For lovers of lean meat, leg is the best choice (it is also slightly easier to carve than shoulder).

To carve either joint you will need a large sharp knife and a two-pronged fork with a thumb guard. Lamb is usually carved fairly thickly and the first step is to locate the largest bone.

For half leg/knuckle end and half shoulder/knuckle end, make a cut down to the bone, then continue to cut slices parallel to this first cut. Turn the joint over and slice the remaining meat horizontally from the bone. Instead of using a fork for this second side, you can hold the shank end of the leg with a cloth in your hand.

For half leg/fillet end, carve horizontally round one side of the joint. Rotate the joint and carve the remaining side.

For half shoulder/blade end, carve slices along one side of the bone, then repeat and cut slices from the other side.

2. Remove the lamb and pat dry with paper towels.
3. Heat the oil in a flameproof casserole. Add the lamb and fry for about 5 minutes, until evenly browned. Add the marinade.
4. Sprinkle the meat and marinade well with salt and pepper. Simmer very gently, covered, for 1½ hours until the lamb is very tender. Remove the meat and place in a warmed serving dish. Keep warm.
5. Strain the liquid through a sieve, pressing as much of the vegetable mixture through as possible with a wooden spoon. Return the strained liquid to the pan and add the redcurrant jelly. Bring to the boil and stir until the jelly has dissolved. Taste and adjust the seasoning if necessary. [A] [F]
6. Serve the sauce separately.
7. Serve with a fruity medium red, or a dry red wine.

[A] Cool the meat and sauce and store separately for up to 24 hours in the refrigerator. Reheat the sauce and meat together for about 20 minutes.
[F] Pack the meat and sauce separately. Thaw in the refrigerator, then reheat for 20 minutes.

MAIALE AL LATTE
Pork with coriander

2 pork chops, rinded
1 teaspoon coriander seeds, crushed
1 teaspoon chopped fresh marjoram or ½ teaspoon dried
　marjoram
1 garlic clove, peeled and finely chopped
25 g (1 oz) butter
1 small onion, peeled and chopped
25 g (1 oz) ham, finely chopped
300 ml (½ pint) milk
salt
freshly ground black pepper
To garnish:
coriander leaves or Continental parsley

Preparation time: 15 minutes
Cooking time: about 1 hour

Arrosto di agnello al ginepro; Agnello coi finocchietti

The tricky part of this recipe is keeping the milk at a very gentle simmer to prevent it evaporating. Add a little more milk if you find this is happening and reduce the heat.

1. Sprinkle the chops with coriander seeds, marjoram and garlic.
2. Heat the butter in a saucepan large enough to take the chops in one layer. Add the chops and fry for about 5 minutes, turning once, until golden brown.
3. Remove the chops from the pan and keep warm. Add the onion, ham, milk, salt and pepper and bring to the boil.
4. Return the chops to the pan and simmer very gently, uncovered, for about 35 minutes, until the chops are tender and a skin has formed on the sauce.
5. Place the chops on a warmed serving dish and keep warm. Boil the sauce for 5 minutes until slightly thickened. Pour a little over the chops and serve the remainder separately. Garnish with coriander leaves or parsley.
6. Serve with a dry white wine or a light red wine.

AGNELLO COI FINOCCHIETTI
Lamb with fennel

1 × 450 g (1 lb) boned leg or shoulder of lamb
2 tablespoons olive oil, for frying
1 medium onion, peeled and sliced
1 garlic clove, peeled and crushed
1 × 225 g (8 oz) can tomatoes
150 ml (¼ pint) beef stock
salt
freshly ground black pepper
1 fennel bulb
1 red or yellow pepper, quartered, cored and seeded

Preparation time: 15 minutes
Cooking time: 1 hour

1. Cut the meat into 4 cm (1½ inch) cubes. Heat the oil in a flameproof casserole, add the meat and fry for about 5 minutes, until evenly browned. Add the onion and garlic and fry for a further 5 minutes.
2. Add the tomatoes, stock, salt and pepper and bring to the boil. Cover and simmer for 10 minutes.
3. Roughly chop the fennel leaves and reserve for garnish. Thickly slice the fennel bulb. Add the pepper with the fennel bulb to the pan. Cook for a further 30-35 minutes until the lamb is tender. [A]
4. Garnish with the chopped fennel leaves. [F]
5. Serve with a light red wine.

[A] Prepare up to 24 hours in advance and store in the refrigerator. Store the garnish separately.
[F] Reheat from frozen for 30-40 minutes.

VITELLO AGLI STECCHI
Skewered veal

225 g (8 oz) piece lean veal, e.g. fillet
salt
freshly ground black pepper
2 tablespoons lemon juice
1 small onion, peeled and quartered
100 g (4 oz) ham
sage leaves
2 tablespoons olive oil

Preparation time: 20 minutes
Cooking time: 25 minutes
Oven: 190°C, 375°F, Gas Mark 5

1. Cut the veal into 2.5 cm (1 inch) cubes. Place in a bowl with salt, pepper and lemon juice.
2. Separate the layers of onion. Cut the ham into 2.5 cm (1 inch) wide strips. Wrap a strip of ham around each piece of veal. Thread on to skewers, alternating with the sage leaves and pieces of onion. [A]
3. Place the skewers on a baking dish and sprinkle with oil. Bake in a preheated oven for 25 minutes. Riso ai funghi (page 26) and a Green salad (page 67) make good accompaniments.
4. Serve a fruity medium dry white wine.

[A] Store the prepared skewers wrapped in foil for up to 12 hours in the refrigerator.

When buying veal the flesh should be pinkish-beige with no dark or discoloured patches. Look for meat which is lean and moist with no juice running from it. Cook veal carefully as it toughens quickly when overcooked.

If you can't find boned shoulder of veal for Scaloppine al vermouth, leg, shin, neck or breast will do, although a little longer cooking time may be needed. Pie veal, cut into chunks, is also suitable.

As an alternative to veal, turkey can be used in many recipes. Instead of using veal escalopes or lean veal in Scaloppine di vitello alla valdestana or Vitello agli stecchi, turkey breast makes a good substitute. Buy boneless turkey breasts and slice or cube them, according to the recipe.

SCALOPPINE AL VERMOUTH
Veal with vermouth

450 g (1 lb) boned shoulder of veal, cut into 2.5 cm (1 inch) cubes
25 g (1 oz) seasoned flour
2 tablespoons olive oil, for frying
1 small onion, peeled and chopped
1 tablespoon chopped fresh sage or 1 teaspoon dried sage
8 tablespoons dry vermouth
250 ml (8 fl oz) chicken stock
1 tablespoon lemon juice
salt
freshly ground black pepper
100 g (4 oz) button mushrooms
1 egg yolk
3 tablespoons single cream
To garnish:
chopped parsley
sage leaves, if available

Preparation time: 15 minutes
Cooking time: 55 minutes

1. Toss the veal in the seasoned flour. Heat the oil in a saucepan, add the veal and fry for about 3 minutes, until evenly browned. Add the onion and fry for a further 2 minutes.
2. Stir in the sage, vermouth and stock and bring to the boil. Add the lemon juice, salt and pepper, cover and simmer for 40 minutes until the veal is tender.
3. Add the mushrooms and cook for a further 5 minutes. [A] [F]
4. Blend together the egg yolk and cream until smooth. Remove the veal from the heat and stir in the egg mixture. Transfer to a warm serving dish. Garnish with parsley and sage leaves. Rice or pasta and Finocchi stufati (page 62) makes a good accompaniment.
5. Serve with a fruity dry white wine.

[A] Store the cooked casserole for up to 2 days in the refrigerator. Reheat gently. Continue with step 4.
[F] Reheat gently from frozen and simmer for 10 minutes or until heated through. Continue with step 4.

Variation
Try blade of shoulder of pork as an alternative to veal.

Scaloppine al vermouth; Scaloppine di vitello alla valdestana

SCALOPPINE DI VITELLO ALLA VALDESTANA
Veal escalopes with ham and cheese

2 veal escalopes, about 175 g (6 oz) each
2 teaspoons seasoned flour
1 tablespoon olive oil
15 g (½ oz) butter
50 g (2 oz) Parma ham, chopped
1 teaspoon chopped fresh marjoram or ½ teaspoon dried marjoram
1 tablespoon grated Parmesan cheese
2 tablespoons Marsala
To garnish:
fresh marjoram

Preparation time: 15 minutes
Cooking time: 12-15 minutes

1. Coat the veal escalopes lightly with seasoned flour. Heat the oil and butter in a large frying pan. Add the veal and fry quickly on both sides until golden brown.
2. Divide the ham between the two escalopes and sprinkle with marjoram and cheese.
3. Stir the Marsala into the pan juices and spoon over the veal.
4. Cover with a lid or foil and cook gently for 3-4 minutes until the cheese has melted. Serve garnished with marjoram.
5. Serve with a light dry white wine.

Fritto misto; Scaloppine di vitello al limone

FRITTO MISTO
Deep-fried veal and vegetables

175 g (6 oz) escalope of veal
1 small aubergine
1 small courgette
100 g (4 oz) mushrooms
4 artichoke hearts
25 g (1 oz) seasoned flour
2 eggs, beaten
175 g (6 oz) dried white breadcrumbs
oil, for deep frying
To garnish:
lemon wedges

Preparation time: 25 minutes, plus chilling
Cooking time: 12-15 minutes

To make the dried breadcrumbs, spread fresh bread-crumbs over a baking sheet and place in a cool oven for 30 minutes.

1. Cut the veal into 2.5 cm (1 inch) wide strips. Slice the aubergine thinly. Cut the courgette in half across, then into quarters lengthways to make sticks. Wipe the mushrooms.
2. Toss the meat and vegetables, including the artichoke hearts, in seasoned flour. Dip in egg and coat with breadcrumbs. Chill for 30 minutes to set the coating. **A**
3. Heat the oil to 180°C/350°F or until a cube of bread browns in 30 seconds.
4. Fry the meat and vegetables, a few at a time, for 3 minutes until crisp and golden brown. Drain on paper towels and keep warm while you fry the remainder. Garnish with lemon wedges. This deliciously varied dish needs very little accompaniment except for a salad.
5. Serve with a dry white or light red wine.

A The coated vegetables and meat can be prepared up to 24 hours in advance and stored in the refrigerator.

SCALOPPINE DI VITELLO AL LIMONE
Veal in lemon sauce

350 g (12 oz) veal fillet, thinly sliced
2 tablespoons seasoned flour
1 tablespoon olive oil
25 g (1 oz) butter
2 tablespoons lemon juice
2 tablespoons chicken stock or water
salt
freshly ground black pepper
To garnish:
2 tablespoons chopped fresh parsley
quartered lemon slices

Preparation time: 10 minutes
Cooking time: 8-10 minutes

1. Toss the veal in seasoned flour. Heat the oil and half the butter in a frying pan. Add the veal and cook quickly on both sides until lightly browned. This will take about 2 minutes. Remove the veal from the pan and keep warm.
2. Reduce the heat and stir the lemon juice and stock or water into the pan, scraping down any sediment. Add salt and pepper to taste. Add the remaining butter to the pan, tilting it until the butter has melted.
3. Return the veal to the pan and reheat gently. Transfer to a warmed serving dish and sprinkle with chopped parsley. Garnish with lemon slices.
4. Serve with a dry white wine.

COTOLETTE ALLA MILANESE
Veal chops with tomatoes and marjoram

2 veal chops
salt
freshly ground black pepper
1 egg, beaten
50 g (2 oz) fresh white breadcrumbs
1 tablespoon olive oil, for frying
25 g (1 oz) butter
Sauce:
2 teaspoons olive oil
1 garlic clove, peeled and crushed
225 g (8 oz) tomatoes, skinned and chopped
2 teaspoons chopped fresh marjoram or 1 teaspoon dried
   marjoram

Preparation time: 25 minutes, plus chilling
Cooking time: 30 minutes

1. Sprinkle the chops well with salt and pepper. Coat in egg and breadcrumbs and chill for 15 minutes.
2. To make the sauce, heat 2 teaspoons oil in a small pan, add the garlic and fry for 2 minutes. Add the tomatoes, marjoram, salt and pepper and simmer, uncovered, for 12-15 minutes, until pulpy. A F
3. Meanwhile cook the chops. Heat the oil and butter in a large frying pan. Add the chops and cook for 12-15 minutes, turning once until golden brown and crispy.
4. Place the chops on a serving dish and pour the sauce over, or serve separately.
5. Serve a dry white wine or a light red wine.

A Store the chops and the sauce separately in covered containers for up to 24 hours in the refrigerator.
F Make and freeze the sauce only. Thaw overnight in the refrigerator. Reheat in a pan while coating the chops, and continue from step 3.

PETTI DI POLLO RIPIENI
Stuffed chicken breasts

2 chicken breast portions
40 g (1½ oz) softened butter
50 g (2 oz) ham, finely chopped
1 garlic clove, peeled and crushed
1 tablespoon grated Parmesan cheese
½ teaspoon dried or fresh rosemary, chopped
salt
freshly ground black pepper
3 tablespoons white wine

Preparation time: 15 minutes
Cooking time: 35-40 minutes
Oven: 200°C, 400°F, Gas Mark 6

1. Wipe the chicken breasts with paper towels. Loosen the skin from the breast.
2. Beat 25 g (1 oz) of the butter with the ham, garlic, Parmesan cheese, rosemary, salt and pepper.
3. Spread the stuffing under the skin of each chicken breast and secure with cocktail sticks. [A]
4. Place the chicken in a baking dish, dot with the remaining butter and sprinkle with salt and pepper. Bake in a preheated oven for 30-35 minutes until tender and golden brown.
5. Place the chicken on a warmed serving dish and pour the pan juices into a small saucepan. Add the wine and bring to the boil. Simmer for 2 minutes, taste and add more salt and pepper if necessary.
6. Pour the sauce over the chicken.
7. Serve with a dry white wine.

[A] Store in the refrigerator for up to a few hours.

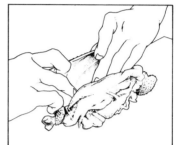
Gently ease away the skin of the chicken breast.

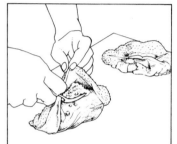
Spoon in the stuffing and secure with a cocktail stick.

POLLO ARROSTO CON PEPERONI
Chicken baked with peppers

2 chicken portions
2 garlic cloves, peeled and crushed
2 sprigs rosemary or ½ teaspoon dried rosemary
2 peppers, 1 each of red, green or yellow, cored, seeded and quartered or cut into 8
1 tablespoon olive oil
salt
freshly ground black pepper
3 tablespoons white wine
To garnish:
Continental parsley

Preparation time: 10 minutes
Cooking time: 50-60 minutes
Oven: 190°C, 375°F, Gas Mark 5

1. Wipe the chicken with paper towels and place in a baking dish. Add the garlic and rosemary.
2. Place the peppers around the chicken and drizzle over the oil. Sprinkle with salt and pepper.
3. Pour the wine into the dish, cover and bake in a preheated oven for 50-60 minutes. After 35 minutes remove the cover to brown the chicken.
4. Place the chicken on a warmed serving dish and surround with peppers. Keep warm. Boil the pan juices and simmer for 2 minutes. Pour over the chicken and peppers and garnish with parsley.
5. Serve with a dry white wine.

POLLO CON SALSE VERDE
Chicken with piquant green sauce

2 chicken breast portions
1 stick celery, chopped
1 carrot, peeled and chopped
1 small onion, peeled and quartered
6 peppercorns
2 cloves
Green sauce:
1 garlic clove, peeled and crushed
1 tablespoon capers, finely chopped
25 g (1 oz) fresh parsley, finely chopped
1 tablespoon wine vinegar
½ teaspoon Dijon mustard
6 tablespoons olive oil
salt
freshly ground black pepper
To garnish:
lemon wedges

Pollo arrosto con peperoni; Petti di pollo ripieni; Pollo con salse verde

Preparation time: 20 minutes
Cooking time: 25-30 minutes

The stock left over is good for soups or sauces.

1. Place the chicken portions in a saucepan with the celery, carrot, onion, peppercorns and cloves. Pour over just enough water to cover.
2. Bring to the boil, cover and simmer for 25-30 minutes, until the chicken is tender. Remove from the stock and cool quickly. Meanwhile, make the sauce.
3. Mix together the garlic, capers, parsley, vinegar and mustard. Gradually stir in the oil, then taste and add the salt and pepper. A
4. Slice the chicken breast thinly and arrange on a serving dish. Pour a little green sauce over each slice and serve any remaining separately. Garnish with lemon wedges. Insalata di fagiolini (page 67) and bread rolls make good accompaniments.
5. Serve with a dry white wine or light red wine.

A Store the cooked chicken for up to 12 hours in the refrigerator. Store the sauce separately.

SALSA DI FEGATINI
Chicken livers with sage and wine

350 g (12 oz) chicken livers
25 g (1 oz) butter
1 small onion, peeled and finely chopped
6 whole sage leaves or 1 teaspoon dried sage
salt
freshly ground black pepper
150 ml (¼ pint) white wine
To garnish:
sage leaves
orange slices, halved

Preparation time: 10 minutes
Cooking time: 15-18 minutes

1. Wash the chicken livers and remove any dark patches or fibres. Pat dry with paper towels.
2. Heat the butter in a small frying pan, add the onion and cook for about 5 minutes until softened.
3. Add the chicken livers and sage and fry for 3-4 minutes, stirring until the chicken livers have changed colour.
4. Sprinkle with salt and pepper and pour in the wine. Bring to the boil, then simmer for 6-8 minutes until the chicken livers are tender.
5. Garnish with sage and orange slices. Gnocchi di patate (page 58) or Riso ai funghi (page 26) and a green vegetable make good accompaniments.
6. Serve with a robust red wine.

ANITRA IN AGRODOLCE
Duck in sweet-sour sauce

2 duck breast portions, completely thawed if frozen
25 g (1 oz) butter
1 large onion, peeled and thinly sliced
200 ml (8 fl oz) chicken stock
1 tablespoon wine vinegar
1 tablespoon honey
salt
freshly ground black pepper
25 g (1 oz) sultanas
1 tablespoon chopped fresh mint
25 g (1 oz) pine nuts
To garnish:
mint leaves

Preparation time: 5 minutes
Cooking time: 1 hour 20 minutes

Salsa di fegatini; Anitra in agrodolce

FEGATO ALLA VENEZIANA
Calves' liver with onions

225 g (8 oz) calves' liver, thinly sliced
salt
freshly ground black pepper
1 tablespoon lemon juice
3 tablespoons olive oil
225 g (8 oz) onions, peeled and sliced
2 teaspoons seasoned flour
4 tablespoons red wine
1 tablespoon chopped fresh parsley

Preparation time: 10 minutes
Cooking time: 20 minutes

1. Sprinkle the liver with salt, pepper and lemon juice and leave to marinate while preparing the onions.
2. Heat the oil in a large frying pan. Add the onions and fry gently for 10 minutes, until softened and lightly coloured.
3. Dust the liver lightly with flour and add to the pan. Fry for about 5 minutes, until lightly browned, turning the liver once.
4. Sprinkle over the red wine, parsley, salt and pepper. Simmer gently for 5 minutes, stirring the onions and turning the liver. Serve piping hot.
5. Patate al forno (page 63) and a green vegetable make good accompaniments.
6. Serve with a light red wine.

1. Wipe the duck with paper towels. Heat the butter in a large saucepan and fry the duck for about 10 minutes, turning until evenly browned.
2. Remove the duck from the pan and add the onion. Fry for about 5 minutes until softened.
3. Add the stock, vinegar, honey, salt and pepper. Bring to the boil and add the duck.
4. Simmer, covered, for 1 hour until very tender. Ten minutes before the end of cooking time add the sultanas, mint and pine nuts.
5. Remove the duck from the sauce and place in a warm serving dish. Skim the fat from the top of the sauce with a spoon and pour the sauce over the duck. [F]
6. Garnish with mint leaves. Gnocchi di patate (page 58) and a Green salad (page 67) make good accompaniments.
7. Serve with a light dry white or light red wine.

[F] Add 1-2 tablespoons water to prevent sticking, and reheat the duck from frozen, simmering it in a covered pan for 10 minutes until heated through. Proceed with step 6.

VEGETABLES & SALADS

ASPARAGI ALL'ITALIANA
Asparagus with egg and cream

225 g (8 oz) asparagus spears
2 tablespoons single cream
2 teaspoons lemon juice
salt
freshly ground black pepper
1 egg
1 teaspoon grated Parmesan cheese

Preparation time: 15 minutes
Cooking time: 20-25 minutes

1. Scrape the stalk ends of the asparagus spears with a sharp knife. Tie in a bundle with fine string and place in a pan half-filled with boiling water. Cover with foil and cook the asparagus for 15-20 minutes until tender. Drain, untie and keep warm.
2. Mix together the single cream, lemon juice, salt and pepper.
3. Pour 2.5 cm (1 inch) of salted water into a small shallow pan and heat to a gentle simmer. Crack the egg into a cup, then slide gently into the pan. Poach the egg for about 3 minutes until the white is just set.
4. Remove the egg with a draining spoon and place on the asparagus. Spoon the cream over the top and sprinkle with Parmesan cheese. Serve hot.

FUNGHI PORCINI AL TEGAME
Mushrooms with mint

50 g (2 oz) butter
350 g (12 oz) small button mushrooms, wiped
1 tablespoon chopped fresh mint
1 tablespoon lemon juice
2 tablespoons red wine or stock
salt
freshly ground black pepper

Preparation time: 5 minutes
Cooking time: 15 minutes

1. Melt the butter in a saucepan, add the mushrooms and cook gently for about 5 minutes, until softened.
2. Add the mint, lemon juice, wine or stock, salt and pepper to the pan. Stir well, then cover and cook gently for a further 10 minutes. Serve hot.

SFORMATO DI PISELLI
Pea puddings

225 g (8 oz) frozen peas
25 g (1 oz) butter
1 small onion, peeled and finely chopped
25 g (1 oz) ham, finely chopped
15 g (½ oz) plain flour
150 ml (¼ pint) milk
salt
freshly ground black pepper
2 eggs, separated

Preparation time: 10 minutes
Cooking time: 35-40 minutes
Oven: 200°C, 400°F, Gas Mark 6

Fresh peas can be used for this dish when they are in season. Weigh them when they are shelled and cook for 10-15 minutes.

1. Cook the peas in a little boiling salted water for 2 minutes, then drain.
2. Heat the butter in a saucepan, add the onion and fry gently for about 5 minutes, until softened. Add the ham and flour and cook for 1 minute.
3. Gradually stir in the milk and cook until the sauce is thickened and smooth. Add the peas, salt and pepper. [A]
4. Remove from the heat and cool slightly. Beat in the egg yolks.
5. Whisk the egg whites until stiff. Stir 1 tablespoon of egg white into the mixture, then fold in the rest carefully until evenly mixed.
6. Divide the mixture between two buttered 450-600 ml (¾-1 pint) ovenproof dishes and bake in a preheated oven for about 25 minutes, until the puddings are risen and golden. Serve immediately.

[A] The sauce can be made several hours in advance and reheated when you are ready to proceed with the dish. Cover it with cling film and store in the refrigerator.

Sformato di piselli; Asparagi all'Italiana

GNOCCHI DI PATATE
Potato gnocchi with Parmesan

450 g (1 lb) floury potatoes, peeled
100 g (4 oz) plain flour
1 egg, beaten
25 g (1 oz) butter
salt
freshly ground black pepper
1 tablespoon grated Parmesan cheese

Preparation time: 20 minutes
Cooking time: 25-30 minutes

Gnocchi can be served as a simple first course or with the main course as an alternative to rice or pasta. It is particularly good with game and rich meat dishes such as Anitra in agrodolce (page 55).

1. Boil the potatoes for 15-20 minutes until tender. Drain well and mash finely.
2. Add the flour, egg, half the butter, salt and pepper to the potatoes. Mix well, then turn on to a floured surface and knead lightly.
3. Divide the dough into two pieces. Roll each piece into a sausage about 2 cm (¾ inch) in diameter, then cut into 2.5 cm (1 inch) pieces.
4. Meanwhile, bring a large saucepan of salted water to the boil. Add half the gnocchi and boil for about 3 minutes until they rise to the top. Remove with a slotted spoon and keep warm. Cook the remaining gnocchi.
5. Dot the gnocchi with the remaining butter and sprinkle with Parmesan cheese. Serve immediately.

CROCCHETTE DI SPINACI
Spinach with egg

1 egg, hard-boiled
450 g (1 lb) spinach, washed
25 g (1 oz) butter
grated nutmeg
salt
freshly ground black pepper
1 tablespoon lemon juice

Preparation time: 15 minutes
Cooking time: 10-12 minutes

If fresh spinach is not available it can be replaced with 225 g (8 oz) frozen leaf spinach. Follow the cooking instructions on the packet.

1. Cut the egg in half and remove and reserve the yolk. Chop the white.
2. Wash the spinach well and place in a pan with only the water that clings to the leaves. Cover the pan and cook for 7-10 minutes, shaking the pan occasionally, until the spinach is tender.
3. Drain the spinach and return to the pan with the butter and a sprinkling of nutmeg, salt and pepper. Heat through, then remove from the heat and stir in the egg white and lemon juice.
4. Transfer the spinach mixture to a warmed serving dish and sieve the egg yolk over the top. Serve hot.

Crocchette di spinaci; Gnocchi di patate; Polenta con formaggio

POLENTA CON FORMAGGIO
Polenta with cheese

300 ml (½ pint) water
pinch of salt
50 g (2 oz) quick cooking polenta
25 g (1 oz) butter
2 tablespoons grated Parmesan cheese

Preparation time: 10 minutes, plus cooling
Cooking time: 12-15 minutes

Polenta is made from maize flour. It is a popular alternative to rice or pasta in Northern Italy and goes well with rich, well-flavoured dishes. The quick cooking variety will thicken in 5 minutes, otherwise increase the cooking time to 25-30 minutes.

1. Bring the water to the boil in a medium saucepan. Add a good pinch of salt and the polenta, and cook for about 5 minutes, stirring well with a large wooden spoon, until thickened and smooth.
2. Pour the polenta out on to a damp flat plate and spread until it is 1.25 cm (½ inch) thick. Leave to cool. A
3. Cut the polenta into 1.25 cm (½ inch) cubes. Heat the butter in a frying pan until foaming, add the polenta and fry for about 5 minutes, until browned.
4. Stir in the Parmesan cheese and cook until just melted. Transfer to a serving dish and serve immediately.

A Polenta can be cooked up to 24 hours in advance, covered with cling film and stored in the refrigerator.

CARCIOFI FRITTI
Deep fried artichoke hearts

5-6 canned artichoke hearts
40 g (1½ oz) plain flour
salt
freshly ground black pepper
1 egg, separated
1 tablespoon olive oil
120 ml (4 fl oz) water
oil for deep frying

Preparation time: 15 minutes
Cooking time: 8-10 minutes

1. Drain the artichoke hearts and cut into quarters. Place the flour in a bowl with a good pinch of salt and pepper. Make a well in the centre of the flour and add the egg yolk and oil. Beat lightly, then gradually beat in the water to form a stiff batter.
2. Whisk the egg white until it forms soft peaks. Fold carefully into the batter, using a metal spoon.
3. Heat the oil to 180°C/350°F or until a cube of bread browns in 30 seconds. Dip the artichoke hearts in batter and fry, a few at a time, for 2-3 minutes until golden brown.
4. Drain on paper towels and serve immediately.

FRITTURA DI CARCIOFI DI GIUDEA
Fried Jerusalem artichokes

450 g (1 lb) Jerusalem artichokes, peeled
2 tablespoons lemon juice
2 tablespoons olive oil
1 garlic clove, peeled and crushed
3 tablespoons chopped fresh parsley

Preparation time: 15 minutes, plus cooling
Cooking time: 15-20 minutes

1. Place the artichokes in a saucepan with the lemon juice and enough water to cover. Bring to the boil, then simmer for 10 minutes, until partly cooked. Drain and when cool enough to handle, cut the artichokes into thin slices.
2. Heat the oil in a frying pan, add the garlic and fry gently for 2 minutes. Add the artichokes and fry until they are golden brown and tender.
3. Sprinkle the parsley over the artichokes and mix carefully, ensuring the artichokes do not break up. Serve immediately.

LEFT TO RIGHT: Insalata di Mozzarella e pomodoro; Carciofi fritti; Frittura di carciofi di giudea

CAROTE AL MARSALA
Carrots in Marsala

225 g (8 oz) carrots, peeled
1 tablespoon olive oil
salt
freshly ground black pepper
4 tablespoons Marsala
To garnish:
chopped fresh parsley

Preparation time: 10 minutes
Cooking time: 15-19 minutes

1. Cut the carrots into thin sticks. Heat the oil in a small pan, add the carrots and turn in the oil until they are well coated and heated through.
2. Add the salt, pepper and Marsala and bring to the boil. Cover and cook gently for about 12-15 minutes, until the carrots are tender but still slightly crunchy. Sprinkle with parsley and serve hot or cold. A

A For serving cold, the carrots can be stored in the refrigerator for up to 8 hours. Bring to room temperature before serving.

INSALATA DI MOZZARELLA E POMODORO
Tomato & Mozzarella salad

1 large or 2 smaller tomatoes, thinly sliced
75 g (3 oz) Italian Mozzarella cheese, thinly sliced
4-5 basil leaves, chopped
Dressing:
1 tablespoon tarragon vinegar
2 tablespoons olive oil
salt
freshly ground black pepper
1 garlic clove, peeled and crushed

Preparation time: 10 minutes

1. Arrange the tomatoes and cheese alternately on a serving plate. Sprinkle with chopped basil leaves.
2. Place the dressing ingredients in a screw-top jar. Shake to mix, then pour over the salad. A

A Dress the salad up to 4 hours in advance, cover and chill. Bring to room temperature before serving.

Variation
Replace the cheese with 1 sliced peach and replace the basil with 2 teaspoons snipped chives.

FINOCCHI STUFATI
Braised fennel

---

2 small or 1 large bulb(s) fennel, quartered
1 tablespoon lemon juice
150 ml (¼ pint) hot chicken stock
25 g (1 oz) fresh breadcrumbs
1 tablespoon grated Parmesan cheese
1 teaspoon finely grated lemon rind
salt
freshly ground black pepper
25 g (1 oz) butter

Preparation time: 10 minutes
Cooking time: 40-45 minutes
Oven: 190°C, 375°F, Gas Mark 5

1. Trim off any tough stalks and the base from the fennel. Parboil in salted water, with the lemon juice added, for 10 minutes; then drain.
2. Place the fennel in a buttered close-fitting ovenproof dish and pour over the hot stock. Mix the breadcrumbs, cheese, lemon rind, salt and pepper. Sprinkle over the fennel and dot with butter.
3. Bake in a preheated oven for 30-35 minutes, until the fennel is tender and the topping golden.

FAVE ALLA MORTADELLA
Broad beans with Mortadella

---

750 g (1½ lb) broad beans, podded
1 stick celery, chopped
25 g (1 oz) Mortadella sausage
25 g (1 oz) butter
salt
freshly ground black pepper

Preparation time: 15 minutes
Cooking time: 16-18 minutes

1. Steam the beans and celery for 10-12 minutes, until tender. Drain and keep warm.
2. Cut the Mortadella into matchstick strips. Melt the butter in a pan, add the Mortadella and fry gently for 3 minutes, until heated through.
3. Stir in the vegetables, salt and pepper and cook for a further 3 minutes. Serve hot.

Finocchi stufati; Sedano al forno

SEDANO AL FORNO
Celery with ham and bay leaves

275 g (10 oz) celery
salt
25 g (1 oz) butter
1 small onion, peeled and sliced
50 g (2 oz) slice of ham, diced
3 bay leaves
freshly ground black pepper
150 ml (¼ pint) chicken stock

Preparation time: 10 minutes
Cooking time: 25-30 minutes

1. Cut the celery sticks in halves. Cook in boiling salted water for 10 minutes, then drain.
2. Meanwhile, heat the butter in a saucepan, add the onion and fry gently for about 5 minutes, until softened. Add the ham and fry for a further minute.
3. Add the celery, bay leaves, pepper, stock and salt, if necessary. Bring to the boil, then reduce the heat, cover and simmer for 12-15 minutes, until the celery is tender. Serve hot.

PATATE AL FORNO
Baked potato layer

350 g (12 oz) potatoes, peeled and thinly sliced
1 small onion, peeled and thinly sliced
salt
freshly ground black pepper
grated nutmeg
25 g (1 oz) butter
150 ml (¼ pint) single cream
1 tablespoon grated Parmesan cheese

Preparation time: 20 minutes
Cooking time: 40-45 minutes
Oven: 200°C, 400°F, Gas Mark 6

1. Layer the potatoes with the onion in a buttered ovenproof dish, sprinkling between the layers with salt, pepper and nutmeg and dotting with butter.
2. Pour the cream over the potatoes and sprinkle with cheese. Bake uncovered in a preheated oven for about 40-45 minutes, until the potatoes are tender and the topping is golden brown. Serve hot.

INSALATA DI CICORIA
Chicory with hazelnut dressing

2 heads chicory
25 g (1 oz) hazelnuts, roughly chopped
salt
freshly ground black pepper
1 tablespoon lemon juice
3 tablespoons single cream
1 garlic clove, peeled and crushed
2 teaspoons chopped fresh parsley

Preparation time: 10 minutes

1. Separate the chicory leaves and arrange around a shallow dish.
2. Place the hazelnuts in a small bowl with the salt, pepper, lemon juice, cream and garlic. Mix with a fork, then pour over the chicory. A
3. Sprinkle with chopped fresh parsley.

A Prepare the chicory and dressing up to 3 hours in advance and store in the refrigerator. Dress the salad just before serving.

Insalata di cicoria; Insalata di radicchio

MELANZANE RIPIENE
Tomato stuffed aubergine

1 aubergine
2 tablespoons olive oil
1 garlic clove, peeled and crushed
1 small onion, peeled and chopped
225 g (8 oz) tomatoes, skinned and chopped
½-1 teaspoon dried oregano
salt
freshly ground black pepper
2 teaspoons grated Parmesan cheese
1 tablespoon chopped fresh parsley

Preparation time: 20 minutes
Cooking time: 30-35 minutes
Oven: 180°C, 350°F, Gas Mark 4

This dish also makes an excellent starter served hot or cold. It will not spoil from being kept warm, covered, for up to 30 minutes in the oven, if you are planning to serve it hot.

1. Cut the aubergine in half lengthways. Scoop out the inside, leaving 1 cm (½ inch) of flesh in the shell. Place the aubergine halves in an oiled baking dish and brush the insides with a little oil. Bake in a preheated oven for 15 minutes.
2. Meanwhile, chop the aubergine flesh finely. Heat the oil in a pan, add the garlic and onion, and fry for 5 minutes until softened.
3. Add the aubergine flesh, tomatoes, oregano, salt and pepper. Stir well and simmer for 10 minutes.
4. Divide the tomato mixture between the aubergine shells, sprinkle with Parmesan cheese and parsley. Return to the oven for a further 15-20 minutes. Serve hot or cold. A

A To serve cold, leave the aubergines to cool, wrap in foil and store in the refrigerator for up to 2 days.

INSALATA DI RADICCHIO
Radicchio salad

2 slices bread
5 tablespoons olive oil
1 garlic clove, peeled and crushed
salt
freshly ground black pepper
2 teaspoons wine vinegar
1 small head radicchio
50 g (2 oz) mushrooms, sliced
parsley sprigs

Preparation time: 15 minutes
Cooking time: 6-8 minutes

1. Cut the bread into 1 cm (½ inch) cubes. Heat 3 tablespoons of the oil in a frying pan. Add the garlic and fry for 1 minute. Add the bread cubes and fry for about 5 minutes, until golden brown. Drain on paper towels and leave to cool.
2. Place the remaining oil in a screw-top jar with salt, pepper and vinegar. Shake to mix. A
3. Shred the radicchio finely and place in a serving dish. Sprinkle with mushrooms and the bread croûtons. Pour the dressing over the salad just before serving and sprinkle with parsley sprigs.

A The garlic croûtons can be made several days in advance and stored in a covered container. Store the dressing in the screw-top jar.

INSALATA DI BIETOLA E RAVANELLI
Beetroot and radish salad

225 g (8 oz) raw young beetroot, peeled and finely grated
few onion rings (red onions if possible)
½ bunch radishes, thinly sliced
Dressing:
2 tablespoons olive oil
1 tablespoon red wine vinegar
½ teaspoon mustard powder
pinch of sugar
salt
freshly ground black pepper
1 teaspoon chopped fresh mint (optional)
To garnish:
fresh mint

Preparation time: 20 minutes

Choose small firm beetroot for this recipe for the sweetest flavour.

1. Place the beetroot in a serving bowl and sprinkle with onion rings.
2. Add the radishes to the serving bowl. Place all the dressing ingredients in a screw-top jar and shake until well mixed. [A]
3. Pour the dressing over the salad just before serving. Garnish with fresh mint.

[A] The salad and dressing can be made up to 4 hours in advance and stored separately, covered, in the refrigerator.

A green salad can be a simple, but stunning, side dish. Instead of lettuce as your base, you could use spinach, endive, sorrel, corn salad (lamb's lettuce), or Chinese leaves. For added bite cut slices or tiny matchsticks of chicory, celery, pepper, cabbage, cucumber or lightly cooked green beans.

To finish the salad prettily, sprinkle it with tiny croûtons, sprigs of herbs, grated courgette, or place a spring onion fan to one side. Cut the bulb off a spring onion, leaving a stalk of about 7.5 cm (3 inches). With a sharp knife shred to within 2.5 cm (1 inch) of the white stem. Plunge into iced water for about 1 hour (or leave for several hours).

CETRIOLO AL MIELE
Cucumber salad with honey

½ cucumber, peeled and cut into chunks
salt
2 spring onions, finely chopped
Dressing:
2 teaspoons clear honey
2 teaspoons lemon juice
2 tablespoons olive oil
½ teaspoon chopped fresh marjoram (optional)
freshly ground black pepper
To garnish:
spring onion fan

Preparation time: 10 minutes, plus draining

1. Place the cucumber in a colander over a bowl and sprinkle with salt. Leave to stand for 30 minutes to drain off excess liquid. Pat dry with paper towels.
2. Combine the cucumber and spring onions. Mix the dressing. Stir together gently. [A]
3. Garnish with a spring onion fan.

[A] The salad can be mixed up to 8 hours in advance and stored, covered, in the refrigerator.

INSALATA DI FAGIOLINI
Bean salad with chive dressing

225 g (8 oz) green beans, trimmed
salt
Dressing:
1 tablespoon wine vinegar
3 tablespoons olive oil
1 tablespoon snipped chives
1 garlic clove, peeled and crushed
freshly ground black pepper
½ teaspoon mustard powder
pinch of sugar

Preparation time: 10 minutes
Cooking time: 7-10 minutes

1. Sprinkle the beans with salt and steam them for 7-10 minutes, until tender, but still slightly crunchy. Drain and refresh under cold running water.
2. Place all the dressing ingredients in a bowl and whisk with a fork until creamy.
3. Place the beans on a serving plate and pour over the dressing. [A]

[A] The salad can be made up to 24 hours in advance, dressed and stored, covered, in the refrigerator.

Insalata di bietola e ravanelli; Cetriolo al miele; Insalata di fagiolini

DESSERTS

CREMA DI MASCARPONE
Almond cream with strawberries

25 g (1 oz) caster sugar
100 g (4 oz) cream cheese
1 tablespoon ground almonds
1 tablespoon Cointreau
225 g (8 oz) strawberries, sliced
To decorate:
strawberry leaves, washed

Preparation time: 15 minutes

1. Beat the sugar with the cream cheese until the cheese is soft and creamy.
2. Gradually beat in the ground almonds, then the Cointreau, to make a soft consistency.
3. Spoon the mixture into the centre of 2 flat serving plates.
4. Alternatively, press the mixture into a heart-shaped cutter on a plate. Lift off the cutter, leaving a decorative shape to the dessert. Arrange the strawberry slices around and decorate with strawberry leaves, if available.

A The almond cream cheese can be prepared up to 24 hours in advance. If the mixture becomes too thick with standing, stir in about 1 tablespoon milk.

GELATO AL PISTACCHIO
Pistachio ice cream

2 egg yolks
40 g (1½ oz) caster sugar
150 ml (¼ pint) milk
40 g (1½ oz) shelled pistachio nuts, finely chopped
85 ml (3 fl oz) double or whipping cream
green food colouring
To decorate:
chopped pistachio nuts

Preparation time: 20 minutes, plus freezing
Cooking time: 15 minutes

ZUPPA INGLESE
Chocolate and pear trifles

1 × 225 g (8 oz) can pear quarters in natural juice
4 sponge fingers, broken into pieces
25 g (1 oz) plain chocolate
150 ml (¼ pint) custard
2 tablespoons Marsala
150 ml (¼ pint) double or whipping cream
chocolate curls

Preparation time: 20 minutes, plus chilling
Cooking time: 5 minutes

1. Drain the pears, reserving the juice. Chop the fruit and place in two serving glasses with the sponge fingers. Pour 2 tablespoons pear juice over each.
2. Break the chocolate into pieces and place it in a bowl over hot water until melted. Remove from the heat and stir in the custard and Marsala. Allow to cool, then pour into glasses and chill. A
3. Whip the cream until stiff. Pipe the cream over the chocolate custard.
4. To make chocolate curls, draw a potato peeler over a bar of plain chocolate. Sprinkle over the trifles.

A Can be made up to 2 days in advance and decorated with cream up to 2 hours before serving.

1. Beat together the egg yolks and sugar until pale. Heat the milk until just below boiling point and stir into the egg mixture.
2. Place the custard in a small pan with the pistachio nuts. Heat very gently, stirring, until thickened. This will take about 10 minutes.
3. Remove from the heat and cool. Whip the cream until stiff, then fold into the pistachio custard. Add a few drops of green colouring. Pour into a shallow container and freeze for about 1½ hours.
4. Transfer to a larger bowl and beat the ice cream.
5. Return to the container and freeze for 1½-2½ hours, until firm. F

F Transfer the ice cream to the refrigerator 30 minutes before serving it.

Crema di mascarpone; Gelato al pistacchio

MACEDONIA DI FRUTTA
Italian fruit salad

---

2 oranges
½ lemon
1 firm ripe pear or 1 apple, peeled
100 g (4 oz) apricots
1 peach
50 g (2 oz) grapes
2 tablespoons Maraschino or Kirsch
1 tablespoon caster sugar
granulated sugar
pink food colouring
1 small banana

Preparation time: 20 minutes, plus marinating

The fruits you choose for this salad will naturally depend on what is in season. Avoid soft fruits, apart from cherries, as strawberries and similar fruits tend to collapse when marinated.

1. Squeeze the juice from the oranges into a bowl. Finely grate the lemon rind and squeeze the juice. Add to the bowl.

2. Quarter and core the apple or pear. Cut into small cubes. Stone the apricots and peach and cut into cubes. Halve the grapes and remove the pips.

3. Add the fruit to the bowl and stir in the liqueur and caster sugar. Place a small plate over the fruit salad to ensure that it is submerged. Marinate in the refrigerator for 3 hours, or overnight. [A]

4. Sprinkle a layer of granulated sugar over a plate. Add a few drops of pink food colouring and stir until evenly coloured. Have ready a plate of water.

5. Dip the rims of two large serving glasses in water, then dip them quickly in the sugar.

6. Slice the banana into the fruit salad and spoon carefully into the prepared serving dishes.

[A] The fruit salad can be marinated for up to 48 hours if necessary. Do not add the banana until just before you are ready to serve it.

IL DIPLOMATICO
Rum and chocolate desserts

---

100 g (4 oz) Madeira cake or plain sponge cake
2 tablespoons dark rum
120 ml (4 fl oz) strong black coffee
1 tablespoon caster sugar
50 g (2 oz) plain chocolate
1 egg, separated
150 ml (¼ pint) double or whipping cream
To decorate:
a few slices of crystallized fruit

Preparation time: 25 minutes, plus overnight chilling
Cooking time: 5 minutes

1. Slice the cake thinly. Lightly butter 2 small bowls or large cups. Line the bowls with cake, cutting the pieces to fit. Reserve enough cake to cover the bowls.
2. Mix together the rum, coffee and sugar. Sprinkle over the cake in the bowls, reserving a little for later.
3. Melt the chocolate in a bowl over simmering water. Remove from the heat, cool slightly and stir in the egg yolk. Whisk the egg white and fold into the chocolate. Pour into the bowls.
4. Cover the mousse with the cake and sprinkle with the reserved coffee liquid. Chill overnight. A
5. Whip the cream until stiff. Turn out the desserts on to serving plates and cover with piped rosettes of cream. Decorate the top with crystallized fruit.

A Store in the refrigerator for up to 2 days, or decorate and store for up to 2 hours.

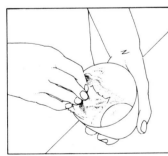
Butter small bowls or large cups.

Fit the slices of cake inside.

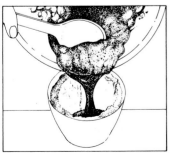
Pour in the chocolate mixture.

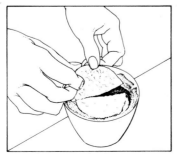
Fit in the reserved cake, to cover.

ARANCE AL CURAÇAO
Marinated oranges in curaçao

3 oranges
2 tablespoons caster sugar
1 tablespoon lemon juice
3 tablespoons curaçao or Cointreau

Preparation time: 15 minutes, plus marinating
Cooking time: 5 minutes

1. Thinly pare the rind from half an orange, using a potato peeler. Cut the rind into thin strips and place these in a pan with a little water. Simmer for 5 minutes, then drain and refresh under cold water.
2. Using a sharp knife, remove the rind and white pith from the three oranges. Cut the fruit into thin slices and place in a serving dish with the strips of orange rind.
3. Sprinkle over the caster sugar, lemon juice and liqueur, turning the orange slices to mix them. Cover with cling film and marinate the oranges in the refrigerator for at least 2 hours, or overnight.

To remove orange rind and pith easily, score the orange in four sections. Plunge the oranges in boiling water for about 30 seconds.

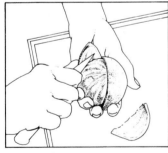

Using a knife, peel off the sections, taking off as much of the pith as possible.

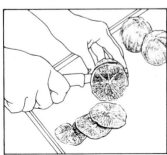

Using a small, sharp knife, cut the oranges into neat slices.

PERE AFFOGATE A MARSALA
Pears poached in Marsala and orange

2-3 firm ripe pears
25 g (1 oz) butter
3 tablespoons Marsala
3 tablespoons orange juice
2 tablespoons double cream

Preparation time: 10 minutes
Cooking time: 15-20 minutes

1. Peel and quarter the pears, then remove the cores. Melt the butter in a pan, add the pears and cook gently for about 5 minutes, until the pears are well coated and beginning to soften.
2. Add the Marsala and orange juice to the pan and simmer for 10-15 minutes, until the pears are tender.
3. Remove the pan from the heat and stir in the cream. Serve warm. Ⓐ

Ⓐ The pears can be cooked the previous day and reheated gently for about 5 minutes.

GRANITA DI ARANCIA
Orange sorbet

2 large oranges
50 g (2 oz) granulated sugar
2 tablespoons water
1 egg white (size 5 or 6)
25 g (1 oz) caster sugar
To decorate:
mint leaves

Preparation time: 20 minutes, plus freezing
Cooking time: 8 minutes

If there's more sorbet than will fit in the orange cases, it can be kept in the freezer for another occasion.

1. Cut the tops off the oranges and scoop out the flesh, using a teaspoon or grapefruit knife. Do this over a bowl to catch the juice. Wrap the orange cases in cling film and chill until ready for use.
2. Press the orange pulp and juice through a large meshed sieve. Place the granulated sugar and water in a small pan and bring slowly to the boil, stirring until the sugar is dissolved. Boil for 5 minutes, then stir in the orange pulp and remove from the heat.
3. When the orange mixture is cool, pour it into a shallow tray and freeze for 2-3 hours, until softly frozen.
4. Whisk the egg white until stiff, then whisk in the caster sugar. Place the softly frozen orange mixture into a chilled bowl and break down with a fork. Whisk in the meringue mixture.
5. Return the sorbet to the freezer for about 2 hours, until frozen. Spoon the mixture into the orange cases to serve. Decorate with mint leaves. F

F The sorbet-filled oranges can be stored in the freezer for up to 1 month. Transfer to the refrigerator 30 minutes before you wish to serve them.

Pere affogate a Marsala; Granita di arancia

Granita di fragole; Gelato all'Amaretto

GRANITA DI FRAGOLE
Strawberry water ice

225 g (8 oz) strawberries
2 tablespoons orange juice
75 g (3 oz) sugar
4 tablespoons water

Preparation time: 15 minutes, plus freezing
Cooking time: 10 minutes

When strawberries are out of season, frozen ones can be substituted, although the flavour will not be quite so fresh.

1. Press the strawberries through a sieve, using a wooden spoon. Stir in the orange juice.
2. Gently heat the sugar and water, stirring, until the sugar has dissolved. Boil for 5 minutes, until syrupy. Cool, then stir into the strawberry pulp.
3. Pour the strawberry mixture into a shallow container and freeze for 3-4 hours, until firm. [F]

[F] Transfer the water ice to the refrigerator 30 minutes before serving it.

Variation:
Granita di pesche (Peach water ice). Peel and remove stones from 2 ripe peaches. Press the peaches through a sieve or blend to a pulp. Add to the sugar syrup and freeze as above.

GELATO AL CAFFE
Coffee ice cream

2 egg yolks
50 g (2 oz) caster sugar
150 ml (¼ pint) milk
25 g (1 oz) coffee beans
150 ml (¼ pint) double or whipping cream
Frosted rose petals (optional):
rose petals
1 egg white, lightly beaten
caster sugar

Preparation time: 20 minutes, plus freezing
Cooking time: 25 minutes

1. Beat together the egg yolks and sugar until pale. Heat the milk with the coffee beans until just below boiling point, then beat into the egg yolk mixture.
2. Place the bowl over a pan of simmering water and cook, stirring occasionally, until the custard is thickened and smooth. This will take about 20 minutes.
3. Strain the custard into a clean bowl and cool. Ⓐ
4. Whip the cream and fold into the custard. Pour the mixture into a shallow tray and freeze for about 3 hours, until firm. Ⓕ
5. To make frosted rose petals, first choose perfect petals. Gently wash them and dry them on paper towels. Brush each one with lightly beaten egg white, then toss in caster sugar. Place on a sheet of non-stick silicone paper or greaseproof paper for about 1 hour, until dried.
6. Serve the ice cream decorated with frosted petals.

Ⓐ Store in the refrigerator for up to 2 days.
Ⓕ Transfer the ice cream to the refrigerator 30 minutes before serving.

GELATO ALL'AMARETTO
Amaretto ice bombe

25 g (1 oz) Italian macaroons, crushed
2 tablespoons Amaretto liqueur
300 ml (½ pint) vanilla ice cream
150 ml (¼ pint) double or whipping cream
1 crushed macaroon

Preparation time: 15 minutes, plus freezing

Choose a good quality firm ice cream to make this bombe, or make your own, following the recipe for Gelato al caffè (above). Omit the coffee beans and add a vanilla pod to the milk. Italian macaroons are sold loose or wrapped in twos (see page 78).

1. Mix together the macaroons and liqueur. Place a circle of greaseproof paper in the base of a wetted 600 ml (1 pint) basin. Chill the basin.
2. Press a little ice cream over the base of the basin. Spread half the macaroon mixture over the top. Cover with a layer of ice cream, then the remaining macaroon mixture. Spread the remaining ice cream over the top. Place in the freezer for 1 hour.
3. Remove the bombe and whip the cream until stiff. Turn out the bombe on to a chilled plate and cover with cream. Ⓕ
4. Sprinkle the top with crushed macaroon and return to the freezer for 15 minutes.

Ⓕ Transfer to the refrigerator for 30 minutes before serving and sprinkle with crushed macaroon.

MONTE BIANCO
Chestnut purée with cream

175 g (6 oz) canned chestnut purée
2 tablespoons dark rum
25 g (1 oz) icing sugar
Topping:
4 tablespoons double or whipping cream
1 teaspoon caster sugar
1 teaspoon dark rum
a little plain chocolate, grated

Preparation time: 15 minutes, plus chilling

Any left over chestnut purée can be used for stuffing, or frozen for another time.

1. Beat the chestnut purée until smooth. Mix in the rum and icing sugar. Divide between two glasses.
2. Whip the cream until it just holds its shape. Fold in the sugar and rum. Swirl on to the chestnut purée and chill until ready to serve.
3. Outline the swirl of cream with grated chocolate. Ⓐ

Ⓐ This dessert can be made several hours in advance and stored in the refrigerator.

ZABAGLIONE FREDDO
Cold zabaglione

2 egg yolks
25 g (1 oz) caster sugar
85 ml (3 fl oz) Marsala
3 tablespoons double or whipping cream
To serve:
Italian macaroons or sponge fingers

Preparation time: 25 minutes, plus cooling and chilling
Cooking time: 10-15 minutes

1. Place the egg yolks and sugar in a bowl and whisk for about 5 minutes, until pale and frothy. Whisk in the Marsala and place the bowl over a saucepan of just simmering water.
2. Whisk the zabaglione for 10-15 minutes, until it starts to become thickened, then remove from the heat and leave to cool, whisking occasionally.
3. Whip the cream until it just holds its shape, then fold into the cooled zabaglione. Divide the mixture between two glasses and chill until ready to serve. Ⓐ
4. Serve with macaroons or sponge fingers.

Ⓐ Keep for up to 24 hours in the refrigerator.

MOUSSE MOCHA
Mocha mousse

2-6 rose leaves
75 g (3 oz) plain chocolate
2 eggs, separated
2 tablespoons strong black coffee
150 ml (¼ pint) double or whipping cream
25 g (1 oz) caster sugar

Preparation time: 25 minutes
Cooking time: 5 minutes

1. Gently wash the rose leaves and allow them to dry on paper towels.
2. Break up the chocolate and place in a bowl over a pan of simmering water. When melted remove from the heat.
3. Brush the shiny side of the rose leaves lightly with oil. Dip each leaf into the melted chocolate to cover it evenly and leave to set.
4. Stir the egg yolks and coffee into the chocolate. Whip half the cream with the sugar until stiff. Fold into the chocolate mixture.
5. Whisk the egg whites until stiff and fold into the chocolate mousse, cutting through until evenly mixed. Pour into a serving dish. Ⓐ
6. Peel the leaves carefully from the chocolate. Whip the remaining cream until stiff and pipe on to the mousse. Decorate with chocolate leaves.

Ⓐ The undecorated mousse can be stored in the refrigerator for up to 2 days.

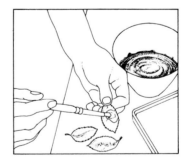
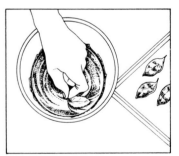

Paint the shiny side of each leaf with oil.

Dip the oiled side into the melted chocolate.

When set, gently peel the leaves away from the chocolate.

Monte Bianco; Zabaglione freddo; Mousse mocha

PESCHE ALLA PIEMONTESE
Baked peaches with macaroons

---

3 firm peaches, halved and stoned
50 g (2 oz) Italian macaroons, crushed
25 g (1 oz) caster sugar
25 g (1 oz) softened butter
1 egg yolk

Preparation time: 10 minutes
Cooking time: 25-30 minutes
Oven: 180°C, 350°F, Gas Mark 4

Italian macaroons have a deliciously distinctive almond flavour. They are sold loose in boxes or wrapped in paper in twos. The paper-wrapped ones have the strongest flavour.

1. Scoop out a little flesh from the centre of each peach half and place in a bowl.
2. Mash the peach flesh with the macaroons, sugar, butter and egg yolk.
3. Place the peach halves, cut side up, in a buttered ovenproof dish. Spoon a little macaroon mixture in the centre of each.
4. Bake in a preheated oven for 25-30 minutes until the peaches are tender and the filling is golden. Serve warm.

BUDINO DI PANE CARAMELLATO
Caramel bread pudding

50 g (2 oz) granulated sugar
1 tablespoon water
50 g (2 oz) dried white breadcrumbs
25 g (1 oz) butter
25 g (1 oz) sultanas
175 ml (6 fl oz) milk
50 g (2 oz) caster sugar
25 g (1 oz) pine nuts
2 tablespoons dark rum
2 eggs, separated

Preparation time: 25 minutes
Cooking time: 1½ hours
Oven: 160°C, 325°F, Gas Mark 3

To make the dried breadcrumbs, spread fresh bread-crumbs over a baking sheet and place in a cool oven for 30 minutes.

1. Lightly oil a 900 ml (1½ pint) charlotte tin or a round cake tin.
2. Place the granulated sugar and water in a small heavy pan and heat gently, stirring, until the sugar has dissolved. Stop stirring and boil for about 5 minutes, until the caramel is golden brown. Remove from the heat and pour into the prepared tin, tilting it to cover the base evenly.
3. Place the breadcrumbs, butter and sultanas in a bowl. Bring the milk to the boil and pour over the crumbs. Stir to melt the butter, then stir in the sugar, pine nuts, rum and egg yolks. Mix well.
4. Whisk the egg whites until stiff, then fold carefully into the crumb mixture. Pour into the prepared tin and place in a roasting tin half filled with hot water.
5. Bake in a preheated oven for about 1¼ hours, until firm to the touch. Leave in the tin until completely or almost cold.
6. To remove from the tin, loosen the edges of the pudding with the tip of a knife, then invert on to a serving plate. [A]

[A] The pudding can be made the day before. Do not chill it. The flavour is best when served at room temperature or slightly warm.

TORTA DI ALBICOCCHE
Fresh apricot tart

100 g (4 oz) plain flour
50 g (2 oz) butter
50 g (2 oz) caster sugar
1 teaspoon grated lemon rind
vanilla essence
1 egg yolk
1 teaspoon water
Filling:
225 g (8 oz) fresh apricots
50 g (2 oz) caster sugar
1 tablespoon water

Preparation time: 25 minutes, plus chilling
Cooking time: 30-35 minutes
Oven: 200°C, 400°F, Gas Mark 6

When apricots are out of season, use a can of apricots in natural juice, drained, and omit the initial cooking.

1. Place the flour in a bowl. Add the butter, cut into small pieces and rub in until the mixture resembles fine breadcrumbs.
2. Stir in the sugar and lemon rind. Add a few drops of vanilla essence, the egg yolk and water. Mix lightly to form a firm dough. Knead lightly on a floured surface, then chill for 30 minutes.
3. Halve and stone the apricots and place in a pan with half the sugar and the water. Simmer for 5 minutes until the apricots are beginning to soften. Remove from the heat.
4. Roll out the dough and line a 15 cm (6 inch) flan tin. [A] [F]
5. Arrange the drained apricots in the pastry case and sprinkle with the remaining sugar.
6. Bake in a preheated oven for 25-30 minutes until the pastry is golden brown and the apricots are tender. Serve warm or cold.

[A] The pastry case can be stored in the refrigerator for up to 3 days before baking.
[F] The pastry case can be frozen for up to 3 months. Cook from frozen, allowing an extra 5 minutes' cooking time.

> To line a flan ring neatly, roll out the pastry carefully. Using the rolling pin to support it, lift the pastry on to the flan ring. Press the dough well into the corners to prevent it shrinking too much. Roll the rolling pin firmly over the flan to trim off the excess pastry.

CLOCKWISE FROM TOP: Budino di pane caramellato; Torta di albicocche; Pesche alla piemontese

INDEX